PRAISE FOR

Well Enough Alone

"[Traig] . . . makes illness seem funny. Her joie de vivre is delicious, even devilish (see her hypochondria haiku). It becomes clear that finding the ability to laugh is the point. After all, if the human imagination can conjure up honest-to-god lip sores, then we'd best learn to laugh when we whip out the Vaseline."　　　　　　　　　　　　　　　—*Los Angeles Times*

"Painfully frank and very funny . . . Traig's brutally honest and wickedly funny voice carries the story. She gives her readers an unflinching look at her physical imperfections without a trace of self-pity."　　　　　　　　　　　　　　—Associated Press

"Generously researched and vividly rendered."　　　　—*Elle*

"Charming, quick, and very funny—akin to pulling off a hilarious literary dissection of a subject that doesn't exactly scream out for one . . . The book's greatness, then, rests in how smoothly it goes down. For a few hours, the reader has a great time and forgets sorrow, an excellent prescription for the uncured hypochondriac in us all."　　　—*San Francisco Chronicle*

"The always-funny Jennifer Traig exposes her tendency to imagine she has been stricken by life-threatening diseases."
　　　　　　　　　　　　　　　　　　　—*Chicago Tribune*

"Who knew life as a hypochondriac could be so witty and hilarious? You'll be reading it out loud to your beach blanket buddies."　　　　　　　　　　　　　　　　　—*Glamour*

"Jennifer Traig makes me sick. At least, that's what I thought until I went to the doctor. It turns out that her funny, fascinating, and heartfelt book about her own hypochondria is not the reason I have this terrible rash. Instead, *Well Enough Alone* merely gave me enormous reading pleasure from a beguilingly smart and perfectly healthy writer."

—John Hodgman, author of *The Areas of My Expertise*

"You will laugh. Then you will feel guilty for laughing. Then you'll laugh some more. Then feel more guilt. Jennifer Traig writes about her illness (and her many perceived illnesses) with such humor, intelligence and poignancy that I'm almost happy she went through it. And now I feel guilty again."

—A. J. Jacobs, author of *The Know-It-All* and
The Year of Living Biblically

"Fellow sufferers will find it a stitch."   —*People*

"If you secretly imagine your funeral when you go to get a mole checked out, read this book. You are probably normal. Jennifer Traig, not as much, but this uncomfortably funny exploration of her hypochondria makes me so glad she never really had the myocardial infarction or the aneurysm or the breast cancer or the alien hand syndrome."

—Beth Lisick, author of *Everybody into the Pool*
and *Helping Me Help Myself*

"A healthy dose of hilarity."   —DailyCandy

"Despite what the hilarious, neurotic, hypochondriac voice inside her head is telling her, there is absolutely nothing wrong with Jennifer Traig's heart, her brain, or her hilariously askew vision. *Well Enough Alone* is a funny, paranoid, intelligent, charmingly eccentric, and ultimately comforting story of hypochondria."   —Dan Kennedy, author of
Loser Goes First and *Rock On*

"I suffer from eight or nine of the same tragic diseases that Jennifer Traig has, and her deeply funny and perceptive book has given me the courage to heal from at least, like, three of them. She's written a smart, thorough encyclopedia of her worst fears—and ours—and the results are hilarious."

—Wendy McClure, author of *I'm Not the New Me*

"Blending . . . medical history with hilarious anecdotes about her own unsavory illnesses, real or imagined, Traig creates a self-poking, sympathetic memoir . . . Traig can write winningly about the ten-pound weight of her oversized breasts or home stool collection and still be charmingly witty. She savors the attention that being sick accords her, though the cure-all Prozac has robbed her of her complaints and granted her the unthinkable: health and happiness."   —*Publishers Weekly*

ALSO BY JENNIFER TRAIG

Devil in the Details:
Scenes from an Obsessive Girlhood

WELL ENOUGH ALONE

A Cultural History of My Hypochondria

Jennifer Traig

RIVERHEAD BOOKS
New York

RIVERHEAD BOOKS
Published by the Penguin Group
Penguin Group (USA) Inc.
375 Hudson Street, New York, New York 10014, USA
Penguin Group (Canada), 90 Eglinton Avenue East, Suite 700, Toronto, Ontario M4P
2Y3, Canada (a division of Pearson Penguin Canada Inc.)
Penguin Books Ltd., 80 Strand, London WC2R 0RL, England
Penguin Group Ireland, 25 St. Stephen's Green, Dublin 2, Ireland
(a division of Penguin Books Ltd.)
Penguin Group (Australia), 250 Camberwell Road, Camberwell, Victoria 3124, Australia
(a division of Pearson Australia Group Pty. Ltd.)
Penguin Books India Pvt. Ltd., 11 Community Centre, Panchsheel Park,
New Delhi—110 017, India
Penguin Group (NZ), 67 Apollo Drive, Rosedale, North Shore 0632, New Zealand
(a division of Pearson New Zealand Ltd.)
Penguin Books (South Africa) (Pty.) Ltd., 24 Sturdee Avenue, Rosebank,
Johannesburg 2196, South Africa

Penguin Books Ltd., Registered Offices: 80 Strand, London WC2R 0RL, England

Throughout this book, the names of some places as well as individuals and their
personal details have been changed.

The publisher does not have any control over and does not assume any responsibility
for author or third-party websites or their content.

All images except "Compression of Arteries" are from Robert W. Taylor, *A Clinical Atlas
of Venereal & Skin Diseases* (Philadelphia: Lea Brothers & Co., 1889).
"Compression of Arteries," by Nicolas Henri Jacob, is from Jean Baptiste Marc
Bourgery's *Atlas of Anatomy*, originally published in 1831.

Copyright © 2008 Jennifer Traig
Cover design © 2008 Kelly Blair
Cover photograph © 2008 Jon Shireman
Book design by Amanda Dewey

First Riverhead hardcover edition: July 2008
First Riverhead trade paperback edition: July 2009
Riverhead trade paperback ISBN: 978-1-59448-380-6

The Library of Congress has catalogued the Riverhead hardcover edition as follows:

Traig, Jennifer.
   Well enough alone: a cultural history of my hypochondria / Jennifer Traig.
      p.   cm.
   ISBN 978-1-59448-991-4
1. Traig, Jennifer.   2. Hypochondria—Patients—Biography.
3. Hypochondria—Humor.   I. Title.
RC552.H8T73   2008   2008005814
616.85'250092—dc22
[B]

PRINTED IN THE UNITED STATES OF AMERICA

10   9   8   7   6   5   4   3   2   1

For my father

Contents

❖

WELL ENOUGH ALONE

I.

Well Enough Alone

❁

I had my first heart attack when I was eighteen. I was striding across campus when it hit, like a bomb going off in my chest. My left arm went numb and it got harder and harder to breathe. I was used to being sick—by the time I started college, I'd already had skin cancer, meningitis, pancreatitis, and blood poisoning—but this was a whopper, and I was knocked over by the crushing pain. This was different. This could kill me, *kaboom*, right there on the quad.

I had to get to a hospital. I still don't know how I got to the student clinic, how I got across the campus and up the stairs. Somehow, I staggered through the double doors and collapsed into a chair.

"I'm having a myocardial infarction," I gasped, when I was finally ushered into an exam room. "Heart attack," I added, when this failed to produce a crash cart.

"I know what a myocardial infarction is," the nurse said, casually taking my vitals. "You're not having one." She pressed a stethoscope to my chest.

"Well, it could be a stroke," I conceded.

"You're not having a stroke."

"I think we should run some tests."

"Haven't we seen you in here before?"

"Once or twice."

The nurse stood up and placed her stethoscope in her pocket. "You're *fine*," she said. "Your vitals are normal. You're a perfectly healthy eighteen-year-old girl. I promise you're fine. Go out, take a walk. It's a gorgeous day and you're not dying."

It was a gorgeous day and I wasn't dying. I'd been spared, by fate or just dumb luck. This, too, had happened many times before. The skin cancer turned out to be ballpoint ink; the meningitis, hay fever; the pancreatitis, too many candy bars; the blood poisoning, ill-fitting shoes. I did not have lupus, multiple sclerosis, Huntington's disease or Hodgkin's, Crohn's disease, diabetes, myelitis, or muscular dystrophy.

What I *did* have was hypochondria, which meant that every other disease was inevitable. I might have escaped the heart attack and the Hodgkin's, but surely something serious was only a matter of time. I could not leave well enough alone, and once dengue fever was ruled out I would return with malaria. There were just so many diseases out there, all strange and for the most part unavoidable. There was, for instance, foreign accent syndrome, the bizarre but real neurological condition that transformed native West Virginians into Eliza Doolittle overnight. There was *pibloktoq*, a seizure condition common to Greenland Eskimos, that compels them do things like destroy furniture, disrobe, scream obscenities, and eat feces.

There was SUDS, the mysterious disorder that claimed healthy young Asian men in their sleep, and even though I was neither Asian nor male, my father had been born in China, so who's to say I couldn't catch it from him. You could catch lots of things. Maybe you'd get paragonimiasis, and parasites would eat you; or you'd get pica, and you'd eat them. Anything was possible.

It's hard to say when the hypochondria started. I'd been worried about my health for as long as I could remember, the anxiety growing like a tumor, each year introducing a new way to die. There were so many ways to go. Besides diseases, there were poisons everywhere you looked. A whiff of the wrong fumes and you'd have instant brain damage. Mistake the glass cleaner for Kool-Aid—and who wouldn't, they were both blue—and you'd need a new liver. By age four I knew well enough to avoid the skull-branded bottles under the kitchen sink, but what about natural toxins? The local landscaper had thoughtfully mined the front yards of our family-friendly neighborhood with all manner of poisonous plants. My parents had warned us to steer clear of the oleander and holly berries, but sometimes a brush was unavoidable. What if I forgot and stuck my pollen-coated fingers in my mouth? What if I sneezed, openmouthed, and a gust of wind blew a blossom in? It didn't seem likely, but it was possible, wasn't it?

The scariest plant of all, of course, was the family tree. When a fourth-grade assignment required me to compile my own, I took less note of when ancestors died than of what: Did we have a lot of heart disease in our family? Any lupus? MS? How about Hodgkin's?

There was remarkably little cancer, it turned out. Hypochondria, however, was in ample supply. The tendency to fear the worst was right there with our short legs and big feet. I had relatives who couldn't breathe, and others who couldn't swallow, and a number who suffered from vague, lingering conditions that required me to forfeit control of the television when they came to visit and to please not wear the loud shoes. Then there was the musician who was more adept at what doctors drily call the "organ recital," the litany of abstract complaints that is the hallmark of the hypochondriac.

My favorite hypochondriac was a cousin thrice removed who was convinced she had stomach cancer. Sure she was dying, she was too afraid to go the doctor until the pain became completely unbearable. Her stomach tumor was born six hours later. He weighed seven pounds, and they named him Francis.

Who knew what bombs were ticking inside you. Even if you didn't inherit any of the awful genetic diseases, you could always catch something: Ebola or malaria, hepatitis or TB. You could pick up a virus, an environmental disease, an infection, or a parasite. And then there's the endless list of worms, thousands upon thousands, crawling in and crawling out: fluke and flatworm, beef worm and tapeworm, roundworm, pork worm, threadworm, heartworm, hookworm. Worms surpass us in both number and fortitude; several thousand nematodes aboard the Space Shuttle Columbia survived the crash. Worms will certainly eat you when you die and perhaps well before. Pinworms might invade your rectum; flatworms, your bladder.

Guinea fire worm might consume your flesh from the inside out. It could happen. It's been happening for eons. The guinea fire worm, in fact, is what you see in the caduceus, wrapped around the rod. Healers used to slit the skin open and draw the critter out with a stick. Yes. Gross.

Hypochondria is no less disturbing and almost as old. It has existed, in various forms, for thousands of years. Perhaps because it allows you to lie in bed without actually killing you, it has endured and flourished and was taken quite seriously for most of history, enjoying a true heyday in the seventeenth and eighteenth centuries. By the nineteenth century it had started to acquire the stigma it retains to this day. It had become perceived as largely untreatable. It was too physical for psychotherapists, too mental for medical doctors, and it responded poorly to treatment of either kind. What was the point in caring for a patient who wasn't sick, but who would never get better nonetheless? And who wasn't even crazy in a fun way? At least with paranoid schizophrenics you get good stories. But unless you find the symptoms of colon polyps interesting, hypochondriacs are just a bore. There's no glamour in it, no red-carpet charity fund-raisers for it, no celebrity spokespeople. And you couldn't ask for a worse poster boy: its most famous sufferer was Hitler.

Even doctors hate us. Most doctors would rather see a patient with weeping genitals than a hypochondriac, and with good reason. Hypochondriacs are difficult, doubting, backseat doctors who continually second-guess their physicians. Convinced that something is fundamentally, fatally wrong, they are the patients who are angry when the path report comes back benign. They are also outrageously expensive. It's estimated that they cost health-care providers billions of dollars in unnecessary tests, care, and procedures.

The problem, of course, is that sometimes hypochondriacs really do get sick. I do, in fact, have about a million things wrong with me. Besides the hypochondria, which makes me think I have everything, I have a long list of very real syndromes and conditions, and the reason I'm so uncomfortable in my body is, in part, because it's such an uncomfortable place to be. I've had just about every annoying condition that doesn't actually affect your overall health: the nuisance diseases. There's the OCD and the IBS. There are the transient parasthesias, where random parts of my body go numb for no reason at all. I've been afflicted with eczema and allergies; appendicitis, gingivitis, and tendinitis; carpal tunnel syndrome, Bell's palsy, essential tremor, heart irregularities, macromastia, and hypoglycemia. I have skin conditions that make me prone to other skin conditions, and have been treated for scabies three times and ringworm twice in the last three years. I'm legally blind in one eye. I also have really bad hair, and cannot for the life of me understand why Japanese hair straightening isn't a covered benefit.

In spite of all this, I'm essentially healthy. Other hypochondriacs aren't so lucky. Some have the misfortune of being both hypochondriac *and* sick; and sometimes patients who get dismissed as hypochondriacs turn out to be profoundly ill. My father, a surgeon, had a patient whose endless, baseless complaints were vindicated a long time later when new technology finally revealed a well-concealed tumor. Researchers are starting to think that one of the most famous hypochondriacs, Charles Darwin, was not a hypochondriac at all, but was suffering from a never-diagnosed case of Chagas' disease, a debilitating tropical parasitic condition that wreaks havoc on the heart and nervous system. It's theorized that both Nietzsche's and Howard Hughes's hypochondria and general weirdness may have actually been caused by end-stage syphilis. In Key West, a lifelong hypochondriac got the last word when she dropped dead at age fifty; her tombstone reads, I TOLD YOU I WAS SICK.

But most hypochondriacs are just whiners. It's this endearing quality that has earned us a number of unflattering nicknames. In the medical industry we are known as GOMERs (Get Out of My Emergency Room) and turkeys. Because we are also known as crocks and crackpots, physicians will sometimes order a check of our "serum porcelain level."

The more sensitive call hypochondriacs the "worried well." The name is apt. We do, indeed, worry extremely well. We worry consummately and constantly. Hypochondria is, in its own way, a terrible disease. The Merck Manual gives it a 5 percent cure rate. This means that you are far more likely to recover from leukemia, heart failure, or necrotizing fasciitis than hypochondria. A few sufferers have even died of it, most notably the writers Sara Teasdale and Jerzy Kosinski. Both committed suicide when they feared death, by nonexistent illness, was imminent.

Cancer, genetic defects, rare disorders—hypochondria makes every condition contagious. For me, transmission usually occurs through the television. They mention it on the news, and within a few hours I'm pretty sure I have it. A hypochondriac family friend was a champ in this department. Kennedy's back problems, Johnson's gallbladder disease—he had them all. When Babe Paley and Betty Ford were diagnosed with breast cancer my mother was sure he'd have his own biopsy scheduled within days. He didn't, but he did catch Nixon's shingles, and most surprising of all, they turned out to be real.

Recently, it's become more common for transmission to occur through the Internet. The proliferation of medical Web sites has produced a new variant of the disease called, predictably, "cyberchondria." It's becoming increasingly prevalent, as the number of people searching for health information online has gone up dramatically. And some of us are responsible for more than our share of hits. (To qualify as a cyberchondriac, you have to visit a health site six times a month, a number I can hit easily during the commercial break of *Trauma: Life in the E.R.*)

This digital version of hypochondria seems an inevitable mutation, what with the Web and high-strung fruitcake behavior making natural bedfellows. Of course you're going to think about sickness while you're online; you're dodging viruses and working on a *terminal*, for goodness sake. There's a metaphorical connection. A couple of years ago, in a moment of perfect, almost poetic coincidence, my computer was infected with a backdoor virus at the exact same time I was. The computer had W32/Backdoor.LYI, and I had norovirus G11.4-2004, but it seemed close enough.

This new form of hypochondria presents new problems. The Web is loaded with the sort of bad medical advice that led me to treat one rash with a diet of all orange foods, and another with direct applications of toothpaste. Many sites seem designed to enflame the alarmist, with symptom finders that quickly escalate from stuffy nose to sinus tumor.

Today, for instance, I'm in pretty good shape. There's a weird mass inside my cheek, my finger hurts, and my hamstrings are sore. I have a rash on my feet and a mild headache. Twenty minutes on the Internet revealed that I do not have deep vein thrombosis, as I suspected, but I still have plenty to worry about: it appears that I do have bacterial meningitis, and that it's too late to do anything about it. Still, this is a blessing, because it's a faster way to go than the oral cancer that would take me if that cheek lesion were allowed to run its course.

It would be a shame to die now, though, just when hypochondria's reputation is starting to enjoy a boost. In the past few years the stigma has eased just a bit. Perhaps driven by the outrageous costs of treating people who aren't really sick, the medical industry has begun to reevaluate the condition, and has come to view hypochondria as a disease in its own right, just not one that requires MRIs, exploratory surgery, and kidney donation.

It's hard to say what all is behind the change. The Web may have something to do with it, easing the exchange of information. Money is part of it, too, as HMOs look for ways to cut costs and please patients. Patients aren't patients so much as consumers now, and the customer is always right, even if the customer is insisting that the sore muscle is end-stage liver cancer. Or it may just be greater acceptance of neurotic behavior in general. Hypochondria is, in a way, just a logical extension of a larger trend toward self-care, like taking vitamins or getting elective coffee enemas.

Coffee may, in fact, play a role. The last time hypochondria was taken seriously was during the Age of Enlightenment, when hypochondria was both common and chic. Then, as now, coffee was also wildly popular, and it does seem worth nothing that caffeine is a drug that induces both palpitations and manic self-examination.

In the last twenty years, hypochondria has been renamed "somatoform disorder," which is more descriptive of the disease as it's understood today—a condition in which you translate stress, or unhappiness, or too much free time, into actual physical symptoms. The common perception of hypochondria as a condition in which a perfectly healthy person worries himself into a lather over nothing isn't quite right. He's overreacting to something that *turns out* to be nothing. The pain and symptoms are real; they just have no underlying physical cause.

It sure seems like they do, however. Hypochondria is very different from faking sickness to get out of work or military service, and it's not a variation of Munchausen's, where the patient knowingly fakes illness to get attention. Hypochondriacs think they're sick because they really, really feel sick, with symptoms they can't ignore: shooting pains or numbness, hair loss and rashes, fevers and palpitations. For reasons that remain mysterious, the symptoms occur far more often on the left side of the body than on the right.

It's amazing what the mind can produce. Expectant fathers suffering from a somatoform condition called Couvade's syndrome acquire all the symptoms of pregnancy except the actual fetus: morning sickness, weight gain, cravings, even labor pains.

Somatizers can conjure almost anything. Case in point: the jelly bean–size sore that recently turned up on my top lip. I do not have herpes; I do not have mouth cancer; I do not have thrush or impetigo. I did, however, spend the better part of the day on medical Web sites trying to reassure myself of this, a quest that ended, after spending time on a folk remedy site, with me swabbing the sore down with *ear wax*, just to be safe.

What I have is somatoform tendencies, and the other night, when I dreamt of a sore on my lip, my body complied, because I am very, very good at this. I can make my body do things I don't want it to, but am powerless to stop. I can't make diseases, but brother, I can make symptoms, especially if they are disfiguring or embarrassing. I'm a sort of blemish psychic, a pustule savant. I picture the festering sore on my hand, and the next day, it's there. The wart, the broken blood vessel, the ingrown hair: check, check, check. Unfortunately, this only works with deformities. I've also tried to use my somatoform skills to produce prominent cheekbones and shiny hair, but it didn't help a bit.

Somatizers are the masters of the -itis, the unexplained inflammation of this or that. Fractures and tumors are hard to conjure with your mind alone, but it doesn't take much to make something swell up. You'd be surprised. I pull it off all the time. Every few months I wake up with an eye swelled shut, an enormously puffy lip, a rigid fluid-filled hand. Today it's my right ring finger. It is hot and red and throbby, and I'm pretty sure that's pus and not frosting, but I'm not going to lick it and check.

For me, these disfigurements always develop overnight. It's like using an oven cleaner, only instead of waking to a sparkling broiler I'm greeted with swollen nodes and moles suddenly grown suspicious. Nobody likes looking in the mirror in the morning, but I find this act inspires an unusual amount of dread. Besides the normal afflictions of bed-head and crusty eyes, I'm likely to encounter sores, sties, pimples, pox, whatever's been on my mind now on my face.

The good news is that somatoform disorder is fairly treatable. Hypochondria is an expensive disease, but once you stop treating the phantom brain tumors and start treating the hypochondria itself it becomes very cost-effective. Recently it's become clear that cheap treatments like cognitive behavior therapy and Prozac will usually do the trick. CBT works about half the time, and SSRIs, about 75 percent. And if not more effective, they are certainly more fun than seventeenth- and eighteenth-century cures, which leaned toward enemas and worse. John Hill's 1766 I'll-give-you-something-to-cry-about prescription is particularly unpleasant: you'll stop fretting over your imaginary aches and pains, he argues, if you develop honest-to-goodness scurvy; and your bleeding hemorrhoids won't worry you at all once you catch leprosy.

The more modern remedies of CBT and SSRIs are, as it turns out, the same treatments prescribed for obsessive-compulsive disorder, which researchers now believe is a related condition. In some studies, as many as one-third of hypochondriacs reported a history of OCD as well. Being in that one-third, I'm inclined to see the connection. The impulse feels the same. With OCD, I worry about the electrical outlet, and with hypochondria, I worry about the mole, but the exercise is the same, an endless lap around a circuit I can't break.

And there's only one runner on the track at a time. I do not check or obsess when I'm feeling particularly hypochondriacal, and at my obsessive-compulsive worst I didn't worry about my health a bit. Though all sorts of things were going terribly wrong with me—my skin turned orange from carotene poisoning, Bell's palsy paralyzed half my face, eczema and overzealous washing reduced my hands to a mass of weeping sores, and my appendix went—I was perfectly untroubled by it all. A yellowing abscess barely merited a "Huh, that's strange." I had other things to worry about, like my mortal soul and the fate of the world, which, I was fairly certain, depended entirely on my ability to chant a given string of words without messing up. Sure, that lump was something I should probably get checked out, but that would have to wait until my flawless recitation of Psalms one through thirty-nine brought peace to the Middle East.

Now that my OCD has more or less gone away, I've been, you know, dabbling. A short list of diseases I've self-diagnosed since starting this book: MS, lupus, lymphoma, ALS, anemia, diabetes, tuberculosis, AIDS, scarlet fever, staphylococcus, cellulitis, diverticulitis, bleeding ulcer, colon cancer, stomach cancer, hernia, herpes (I and II), hepatitis (A, B, and C), septicemia, stroke, DVT, kidney failure, cirrhosis, hyperthyroidism, hypothyroidism, Lyme disease, and rickets. I've had an MRI, two heart echocardiograms, a four-hour surgery, an EKG, a sigmoidoscopy, a Pap smear, a mammogram, a stress test, and a CT scan. I've been on eight different prescription medications and countless over-the-counter ones. I've given samples multiple times of every fluid my body produces and visited more doctors than I can recall. I've had physical therapy, regular therapy, cognitive behavior therapy, and group therapy; chiropractic, cupping, and acupuncture. And in case my HMO is reading this, I hasten to add that every treatment was medically indicated by real and obvious symptoms, except for the cupping, which was indicated by boredom. All the rest of the symptoms, though, were demonstrable and true: I couldn't feel my arm; I couldn't breathe; I couldn't walk; I was bleeding internally; my heart rate was dangerously high, and I had every indication of a blood clot.

In case my HMO is reading this, I'll also note that in the past year, at least, I've gotten much better. There was exactly one doctor visit, for a very real and completely gross sebaceous cyst. Though I still surf from time to time, I no longer have WebMD bookmarked; and while it's true that I received both a *Physicians' Desk Reference* and *Stedman's Medical Dictionary* for Hanukkah, I mostly use them to diagnose other people.

I'm not entirely sure why things improved. Maybe my hypochondria responded to CBT and SSRIs, or maybe it responded to HBO and MTV—I got really, really great cable, and this has proved a wonderful distraction.

And this, I realize, is part of it. John Hill was right: you don't notice the bleeding hemorrhoid when you get leprosy. You don't notice the boredom and depression and the fear that your life is completely off course when you have a funny twinge to preoccupy you instead. And you don't notice the funny twinge when Meredith Baxter Birney is fighting off both alcoholism and would-be kidnappers on the E! network.

I'm particularly fond of the medical shows. Because I'm still susceptible to infection by TV, I tend to favor shows about conditions I'm unlikely to get: dwarfism, gigantism, inguinal hernias, or that genetic anomaly where you grow a full head of hair on your face.

Just now I noticed a little, pinkish pocket of fluid under my eye. It could be an infection, I suppose, or maybe something deadly bit me in the night. And I could spend the rest of the morning on the Web, on the phone with my doctor or my dad, trying to figure out what it is, and how long I have left. But at eleven, The Learning Channel has a special on the morbidly obese, followed by eight hours of maternity ward emergencies. After dinner, I'll watch a show about Munchausen moms, and another about cataplexy, then go to sleep by the light of plastic surgery disasters.

I'll probably be just fine.

Fig. 1. Ringworm of Head

2

Hypochondria:
The Miniseries

✿

Because it rarely features reality shows about desperate tramps competing for a bachelor, I don't often watch the History Channel, but I'd find my way there if they ever aired a history of hypochondria. It's a long and absorbing saga, and I can't help thinking it would make a fine miniseries. To swelling strings, the camera opens on what appears to be a windblown savanna surrounding a barren hill. In come the drums and spooky flute music. The camera pulls out farther and farther until we realize we're looking at the mysterious spot that started it all, the strange bump on Ogg's leg.

Ogg probes the site as his prelingual grunts are translated to subtitles. "Maybe is same Big Purple Sick killed mastodon. Maybe is curse of Sky Bear for bad thing Ogg do." Ogg furrows his slanted brow. "Maybe is ingrown hair, but probably Big Purple Sick."

Next we see a montage of hypochondriac scenes through the Iron Age and Biblical times, the limping cavemen giving way to robed nomads palpating their abdomens. Cue voice-over as the audience settles in for ten more hours of vaguely swollen nodes, suspected hair loss, fainting spells, shortness of breath, difficulty swallowing, and joint pain.

THE STORY OF HYPOCHONDRIA DOES, in fact, go back quite a way. The term was first coined by Hippocrates in the fourth century BCE, from *hypo*, under, and *chondrium*, rib cartilage, to describe various problems of the spleen, liver, and gallbladder. At this point it was still just an anatomical term. "The lamb isn't agreeing with my hypochondrium," one might say, or "Your hypochondrium looks great in that tunic."

The definition continued to evolve and by the second century, it was starting to resemble the hypochondria we know today. For Galen, it was a condition defined by mood-related stomach trouble. As time went on, it came to include more symptoms, like sleeplessness, irritability, and malaise. Classified as a melancholic disorder, it was thought to have both mental and physical aspects, and was taken rather seriously. It was blamed on an excess of black bile, and was treated with a variety of remedies designed to bring the humors back in balance, including diet, bloodletting, purgatives, and enemas.

This may explain why its popularity waned somewhat in the Middle Ages. Sure, leeches and laxatives were fun for the Dark Ages, but by medieval times there were far more entertaining tortures, like scalding oil showers and Catherine wheels. With so many external methods for mortifying the flesh, hypochondria became unnecessary. Some have argued that it was replaced by *pusillanimata,* a "spiritual hypochondria" scholars have linked with scrupulosity, a religiously oriented form of OCD I was to suffer myself a thousand years later. This variant failed to catch on in any big way, however. As a disorder, it just didn't hold much appeal. I'm not sure if this is due to cultural shifts or to the fact that "pusillanimata" sounds like a particularly virulent vaginal infection.

Toward the end of the Renaissance, hypochondria experienced a renaissance of its own. Like the Renaissance, this originated in Italy, where melancholy and melancholic hypochondria became fashionable among the artistic, self-reflective set. It was our moment in the sun, and it just burns me up that I missed this. The trend proceeded to sweep across Europe, each country claiming the disease as its own. In France it was called *la maladie du français;* in England, the English Malady. By the seventeenth century, Europe was in the grips of a wide-scale hypochondriac chic. The disease acquired a cute nickname, "hyp," and the well-heeled rushed off to spas to treat their vague but fashionable complaints.

There, they were generally treated with the same remedies Galen advised centuries earlier. George Cheyne's prescription in 1733's *The English Malady* is fairly typical: "I know not in Nature a more universal and effectual Remedy for most, if not all the Symptoms of these Disorders when they rise to any high Degree, than gentle *Vomits* suited to the Strength and Constitution of the Patient."

Others prescribed more colorful solutions. The well-known seventeenth-century Jesuit poet Tommaso Strozzi claimed, in a poem, to have been cured of his hypochondria through prayer, and suggested that chocolate might do the trick for others. After much personal experimentation with fun-size candy bars, I can report that this is ineffective, but all in all not a bad way to spend a morning.

It's certainly more pleasant than the hard-line cures offered by the notoriously disagreeable pamphleteer John Hill of the I'll-give-you-something-to-cry-about cure. In *Hypochondriasis: A Practical Treatise*, he offers "Rules of Life for Hypochondriac Persons," which include air and exercise, and warns that a sedentary life will lead inexorably to diarrhea. He also suggests the hypochondriac invite himself to stay with friends abroad. I sometimes like to imagine how these conversations went. "You're planning to stay for how long, exactly? And you're bleeding from where? [Pause.] Well, you can come, but Fanny says you'll have to bring your own chair."

Still, the disease carried no stigma, and sufferers found great inspiration in their lamentable symptoms. While Renaissance artists were forging new art forms, hypochondriacs were discovering new maladies and, like the sculptors and poets, celebrating these in art of their own. This trend died out before the world was forced to endure "Six Couplets on a Bowel Impaction" or "Still Life with Abscess," but not before the hypochondriac Lady Winchilsea lamented her condition in a Pindaric ode entitled "The SPLEEN" ("We faint beneath the Aromatick Pain / Till some offensive Scent thy Pow'rs appease / And Pleasure we resign for short, and nauseous Ease").

Hypochondriac chic reigned well into the eighteenth century and inspired plays and several best sellers. One of the most successful pieces of hypochondriacal literature was Robert Burton's *Anatomy of Melancholy*, a wildly popular four-volume exploration of neurotic unhappiness in all its forms. The book enjoyed eight reprints, which is an awful lot for a seventeenth-century text without nudity or funny parts.

The book is pretty funny now, however, if you, like me, have the maturity of a seventh-grader. Quoting the, uh, classical literature on the subject, Burton lists the symptoms of this "hypochondriacal or flatuous melancholy": "sharp belchings, fulsome crudities, heat in the bowels, wind and rumbling in the guts, vehement gripings, pain in the belly . . . indigestion, they cannot endure their own fulsome belchings, continual wind about their hypochondrias, heat and griping in their bowels . . . the veins about their eyes look red and swell from vapors and wind. . . . And from these crudities, windy vapors ascend up to the brain which trouble the imagination and cause fear, sorrow, dullness, heaviness, many terrible conceits and chimeras . . . (arising to the brain from the lower parts 'as smoke out of a chimney')."

The seventh-grade material is, unfortunately, typical of the genre. Like most modern readers, my ideas about the eighteenth and nineteenth centuries come entirely from Jane Austen, but Austen omits all the intestinal turbulence. It's shocking to consider. Replace Mr. Darcy with Howard Stern or the dad from *The Family Guy* and you'll have a far more accurate idea.

Hypochondria was—sorry—a gas. Its sufferers truly suffered, to be sure, but they were rewarded with sympathy, opiates, and book contracts. James Boswell made a career of it. Most famous for his biography of the profoundly hypochondriacal Samuel Johnson, Boswell also wrote a monthly column called "The Hypochondriack" for *London Magazine* from 1777 to 1783, in which he pondered the trials of contemporary life, including sickness, death, executions, and English cooking.

Boswell's columns weren't nearly as interesting as the worries he confessed in his private correspondence. Therein he frets over various venereal diseases and the condition of his testicles. These concerns were not enough, however, to keep the things tucked away. An enthusiastic patron of London's prostitutes, Boswell managed to contract gonorrhea nineteen times and produce an illegitimate son. The son's death did nothing for Boswell's mental health, which probably wasn't too stable to begin with. Boswell liked to distract himself from his symptoms by watching public hangings. Perversely, these made him randy. Hypochondriac, sure, but I think we can all agree he was sick, too.

Like most hypochondriacs of the time, Boswell was wealthy. The disease, which called for copious amounts of time off and high-thread-count bedding, was mostly an affliction of the rich. As time went on, however, it began to trickle down to the masses. Seamstresses began to complain of light-headedness, farmers and blacksmiths of mysterious aches, moaning and limping like landed gentry. These blue-collar sufferers were attracted to the pampered calm of charity hospitals. There, they enjoyed a diet of laxatives and iron filings, a therapeutic protocol that generally guaranteed a short stay. Off they hobbled, back to work.

Once the disease was available wholesale it became popular among Jews, which explains its presence in my own family history. The I TOLD YOU I WAS SICK tombstone is, unsurprisingly, in Key West's Jewish cemetery (located, and I am not making this up, on Passover Lane. Whether this is a Jewish version of Candy Cane Lane or a bad pun about passing on, I couldn't say).

By the mid-1800s, doctors had coined the term "Hebraic debility" to describe the vague chest and stomach complaints of their Jewish patients. The condition became common enough to justify a study by a Yiddish-speaking Harvard medical student, who concluded that the primary symptom was constipation. Galen blamed the spleen, but I think we can blame kugel. The more philosophical blamed the Jewish temperament and history of persecution. Jews, they argued, needed something to fear. Now that there were no pogroms and very little smiting, they worried about diverticulitis and peptic ulcers.

It was around this time that hypochondria acquired the rest of the trappings it carries today, thanks mostly to Jean-Pierre Falret's influential 1822 treatise *De l'Hypochondrie et du suicide*, which narrowed the definition of the disease to a preoccupation with health. Falret made the then-revolutionary claim that the disorder starts in the brain and not the stomach, and that it was the brain that required treatment. He also said that the disorder was caused by overwork; an excess of sugar, tea, or cold drinks; and masturbation.

Not surprisingly, all this lent hypochondria a certain stigma, and as the nineteenth century wrapped up, hypochondria fell out of both fashion and favor. Freud didn't help matters much. Hypochondria confounded him. Not knowing what to make of it, he largely dismissed it, an oversight he later regretted. It was, he believed, a neurosis with a physical basis, originating in the organs, not the brain. He halfheartedly suggested that it was caused by the body directing its sexual impulses back at itself. And he's right, in a sense, because the hypochondriac does little but fuck himself, wasting his time and energies on symptoms that amount to naught.

Post-Freud, in any case, hypochondriacs were fairly well-screwed. Psychiatrists wouldn't treat it because it was a physical condition; doctors wouldn't treat it because it was psychological. All parties thought it was a waste of everyone's time, a perception that continued until just recently, when the good drugs were invented and things started to change.

And if this were a History Channel miniseries, this is where I'd turn it off; I know what happens next. There's the sore throat, and then the cancer scare, and then the Prozac and the therapy, and then maybe things get better, or maybe they don't. But this doesn't make for very good TV, so instead let's close with a futuristic fantasy. It's the year 3017, and Oggatron-XR is examining his circuitry. He probes at a loose wire as his binary beeps are translated to subtitles. "Perhaps it is time for a new battery. Perhaps all that is required is a reboot." Ogga-tron-XR pauses while data flashes across his control panel.

"It could just be a short circuit. But probably total system failure."

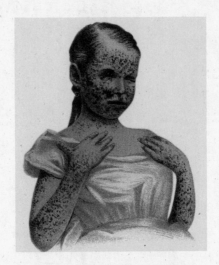

Fig. 2. Xeroderma Pigmentosum

3.

Playing Dead

✼

When I was in second grade, our Halloween art assignment was to draw the scariest thing we could think of. Some of my classmates drew the shark from *Jaws*, some Bigfoot. The more self-righteous drew litter, and a few, frightened by the previous night's network KISS special, drew Gene Simmons.

My best friend drew a ghost. I drew an aneurysm.

After school I took the drawing home to my mother. She leaned against the kitchen counter as she puzzled over the popping blood vessel. My depiction was enthusiastic but clumsy, and I had to explain what it was. "You can see the vein blowing up right there," I said, pointing at the pink splodge in the middle of the page.

It was, in fact, the thing that had killed her own father, and my spirited rendition was perhaps a little insensitive. "What the hell?" My mother frowned, shaking her head. "You're sick all right, but not the way you think." By now the vein in her own forehead was throbbing, and she sent me to my room to think about what I'd done. Instead, I lay on my bed with the curtains drawn, fuming while I resisted the urge to palpate my abdomen for tumors.

She was right, though. I was sick. I worried about things. One of these things was my health, and it troubled me more and more each year. Hypochondria was in my blood. Sure, neither of my parents are hypochondriacs, but they're both in medicine, and it seems worth noting that their first date was to see a production of Molière's *The Imaginary Invalid.*

Of course I drew an aneurysm. Was anything scarier than such a sudden, awful end? Was anything more worrisome than the ominous mysteries of our own bodies? I worried about the head rush I felt on standing, the weird stabby feeling I sometimes got in my neck, the rash on my eyelids, the moles on my legs. At night, the sound of my own pulse distracted me so much—What if it stopped? Was it really supposed to sound like that? Wasn't that last beat a little off?—that my mother made me sleep with her watch on my pillow, its ticks drowning out my own.

But who could sleep, with so many things waiting to kill you, starting the second the day began. There was, for instance, the trip to school, on a bike which routinely tried to eat my leg, or even worse, in the car, as my parents happily allowed us to ride unbelted in a car full of smokers. This was followed by several hours of lead pencil exposure and asbestos inhalation in a classroom whose carpet generated so much static I would sometimes raise my hand to ask if I was being electrocuted. Next was lunch, which required consuming a sandwich that sat unrefrigerated in my cubby for *four whole hours every day,* a risk I was willing to take when said lunch included, say, delicious ranch dressing, but which doubled and tripled when it involved luncheon meat, for its sheer disgustingness. Then came recess, the most dangerous activity of all, on what anyone would have to consider the Playground of Death. I'd seen one classmate bite through her own chin in a fall from the monkey bars and yet another break his arm, exposing bone, actual pearl-white bone, when he went sailing off the swings.

There were a lot of reasons to associate the playground with sickness and physical harm. Even hopscotch couldn't provide a respite, as each square of the hopscotch court was inscribed with the name of a childhood killer: RUBELLA, WHOOPING COUGH, TETANUS. My mother and sister and I were, in fact, the ones who'd inscribed them, as part of a "Stamp Out Disease!" campaign started by my mother's women's group to promote immunization. I like to think there was a similar hopscotch at the junior high with CHLAMYDIA, SYPHILIS, GONORRHEA, but if there was, I didn't know about it.

I had enough to worry about as it was. If I didn't catch something at school I'd probably pick something up at home. There was the stroke that killed my grandfather; the brain tumor that took my grandmother; the cancer, the heart attacks, the Parkinson's. It made you wonder if the family's hypochondriacs weren't crazy so much as paying attention.

I also had a lot of relatives who were doctors, but I had no interest at all in being one of them. The doctors worked all the time. The hypochondriacs napped. The doctors fussed, and the hypochondriacs were fussed over. The doctors gave attention, and the hypochondriacs got it. You didn't have to be a brain surgeon to figure out which was the smart way to go. I did not want to play doctor but patient, and there were no accessories I coveted more than medical supplies. That year, my birthday wish list consisted of crutches, an Ace bandage, headgear, an eye patch, a sling, and a cast.

True pediatric hypochondria is very rare; onset typically occurs in early adulthood. At age seven, I was only on the JV squad, and it would be several years before I turned pro. For now, disease was just one of the many, many things I worried about, a single channel on my full cable lineup of anxiety. I worried that the tomato plants in the backyard would turn carnivorous and eat me. I worried about killer bees and flying monkeys, land sharks and yetis. I worried that nuclear war was imminent. That I'd stunted my growth eating cake mix. That I'd have to go to a second-tier college. That—and this was worst of all—other people, especially my sister, would get more attention than me. And being a little sick conveniently guaranteed that wouldn't happen.

Later that year I'd get to play the Wicked Witch in a classroom production of *The Wizard of Oz*. This was fantastic for two reasons: one, it guaranteed me an audience, and two, I had full creative license. Since I was allowed to choose my own costume and interpret the role as I saw fit, I piled on all the disfigurements I could think of. My witch was a polio victim with advanced gum disease, profound tooth and hair loss, and some skin lesions she should really get checked out. It was more sicked than wicked, but to a budding hypochondriac, still scary in its way.

Normally my parents didn't encourage my imaginary injuries but as this seemed a proper outlet for my impulses, they indulged me. To black out my teeth and make my warts, my mother even let me use her normally off-limits night school art supplies, her charcoals and grease pencils. That these were certainly toxic and had no place in my mouth did not, apparently, occur to me.

I once read that more people are afraid of being onstage than dying. As a hypochondriac, on some level, I have to snort at that: your stage fright is no competition for my necrotizing-fasciitis fright. And hypochondria is, in a way, an affection for the staged, for the imagined and dramatic. I don't know if it's the hypochondriac's fondest wish or worst fear to actually, truly, die in front of an audience. Molière himself nearly managed to in a performance of *The Imaginary Invalid*, the same play my parents saw on their first date. Molière was playing the title role when a tubercular coughing fit resulted in a seizure and hemorrhaging. The legend holds that he died onstage, which is not quite true—it was a couple hours later—but close enough.

At first the audience thought the seizure was part of the show. And in hypochondria, that's partly what the manifestations are, a performance, albeit a command performance you can't control. You're playing a role, stroke victim or diabetic, trying on symptoms like costumes. It's Halloween, a chance to wear a different identity for a while, to experience a scare that turns out to be just that, a scare, and not cancer at all. It's a pageant, and for the duration, the spotlight is on you.

And this is the secret part, the embarrassing part, especially true in children but no less in adults: hypochondria keeps you entertained and entertaining. It gets you attention. Who doesn't, on some small level, envy the boy with the broken arm being loaded into the ambulance, the girl with the perforated chin getting flowers and gifts?

That's not what makes hypochondriacs do what we do, of course—we truly cannot help it—but it's part of what keeps us from stopping. Hypochondria is, in a way, hyperbole, the mountain from the molehill, the melanoma from the mole. Without the hypochondria, all you're left with is a mole, and who's going to be interested in that?

Unless, of course, it's a truly special mole, like the one my Wicked Witch wore: a marble-size carcinoma you could see from the back row. The lights glinted off it during my musical number. Then came the highlight of the show, when Dorothy hosed me down and I got to play dead. It was the role I was made for. I seized like Molière, shuddered out a death rattle, and expired. Everyone was watching and it was glorious. I killed.

Fig. 3. Leprosy

4.

Anatomically Correct

✿

In part because the hypochondria made it seem so fragile, and in larger part because of the aforementioned stumpy legs and big feet, I've hated my body for as long as I can remember. Even at age seven, I had a horror of being naked. A few years earlier I'd been hugely relieved to learn I'd been born wearing a suit.

"Have the neighbors been teaching you words again?" my mother demanded, when I'd asked her about it. "'Birthday suit.' Well, at least it's longer than their usual four letters, I'll give them that."

I'd wanted to know what mine had looked like. Was it double-breasted or three-button? Herringbone or houndstooth? Skirt or pants? Because my mother liked to sew I imagined it must have been finely made, with tiny lapels and a dainty ruff. Maybe we still had it, packed away and preserved for my own children. Maybe there were pictures of me in it, all trussed up like Little Lord Fauntleroy, that I could bring to school for show-and-tell.

"I just wanted to know, is all." I'd shrugged.

"Your birthday suit is your naked body," my mother replied, turning back to her hem.

"No way."

"It's true."

"*No.*"

I'd been horrified. Naked, really? "Did people see me?" I'd demanded. "Did they take *pictures*?"

Born naked. I was appalled. By early childhood I'd done all kinds of embarrassing things, like quizzing strangers about their ethnic background and wiping habits, but this really took the cake. The thought made me frantic, and I would not calm down until my mother assured me I'd been wrapped in a blanket before anyone could get a good look. That everyone else came into the world this way did not occur to me, and I'd made my mother promise not to tell anyone.

"Don't worry, you can still run for office," she'd said, patting my head.

Hypochondria aside, I don't know where this prudishness came from. My no-nonsense parents had taught us there was nothing wrong with the human body. Naturally, my family is embarrassed by nudism, the deliberate kind of nudity that implies an effort was made. It's fine if you're just too lazy to put on pants—we've all been there—but if you've artfully accessorized with a sun visor, a fanny pack, and a thorough basting of sunblock, well, that's just weird. When a family acquaintance announced she had joined a nudist community and was adopting what she called "the natural lifestyle," we were appalled. We pictured her speedboating and playing Ping-Pong in nothing but Reeboks and a straw hat, and we giggled and cringed.

Normal nudity, however, was fine, and on special occasions, graduations and the like, a little public nudity was considered perfectly appropriate. Until recently my sister Vicky and our cousins celebrated New Year's Eve with a naked jog around the block. Vicky was living in a manicured, residential neighborhood at the time, and once a year she needed to blow off a little steam by airing her bare backside. "They're already complaining about the couch on the lawn, might as well give them something more to bitch about." She shrugged.

Before I bring friends to visit her, I sit them down for a warning. "Listen, it's unlikely she'll close the bathroom door, and if it's over seventy degrees I can't promise she'll be wearing pants. Also, unless it's brown, she won't flush it down. So if you're uncomfortable with casual nudity or stale urine you should probably just stay home." But most of my friends are as easy-going as she is, and no one really minds.

I'm the one who can't let it mellow. The naked body, the diseases that might be growing inside of it, and, ugh, the things that come out of it—it just undoes me. Even in museums, I find I can only look at the nude's eyes, as if we were having a pleasant conversation in which I was desperately trying not to notice her exposed nipple or the leaf jutting out of her hoo-ha. I still don't know how I survived the streaking craze of the 1970s. That was worse than ghosts, monsters, aneurysms, or tumors. It was like some perverse form of terrorism. You could be anywhere—a gas station, Wimbledon, the Oscars—and suddenly be confronted with a flapping scrotum or pimply behind.

At the time, the only bodies I was comfortable with were my dolls'. With their perfect plastic anatomies, free of disease and disfigurement, cellulite, and surgical scars, they saw no reason to put on clothes. They were a free-spirited bunch who did everything in the buff—grocery shop, fight crime, mow the lawn. They might throw on a pair of knee-high boots and a beret to go, say, to the beach, but most of the time they were naked as jaybirds.

Because this was the 1970s they were not Barbies but *Charlie's Angels* action figures, all of them acquired at birthday parties against my mother's will. My mother was plainly disturbed both by the show and the scenarios it inspired my sister and me to reenact. It wasn't that she thought the Angels were inappropriate for children; she just thought they were insipid. At one point, she'd tried to distract us with an expensive, finely crafted Black Power doll named Sasha, who was lovely, but could not sustain our interest. After a day or two of naked Black Panther rallies we were back to the Angels, acting out the story of three little girls who'd been subjected to all kinds of danger. I took them away from all that, and now they worked for me.

It was after my mother walked in on us reenacting a recent episode about the Angels' undercover foray into a massage parlor to investigate the murder of an teenage call girl—here played by Sasha—that she decided things had gone too far. "It's just not right," she muttered. "That doll was handcraft-ed in Kenya and here you've got her offering lap dances to a Weeble."

In short order she'd replaced the Charlie dolls with another Charlie doll, and the next thing I knew I was the proud owner of a Charlie McCarthy ventriloquist's dummy.

This was a baffling gift. It was so extravagant. My sister and I knew we were loved, and we certainly never wanted for any-thing, but in general we received gifts of things like pajamas and paperbacks. A ventriloquist's dummy was up there with a child-size Corvette or a home jukebox, something my family just didn't do.

It was also, potentially, very dangerous. My parents wanted me to be a ventriloquist? It didn't make any sense. They were generally only in favor of us pursuing a talent if it was either noiseless or took place in a classroom across town. Knitting was highly encouraged, but when I'd taken up the clarinet, they'd forced me to practice in the backyard. For the first full month of piano lessons I'd had to practice my fingering si-lently on a Xeroxed copy of a keyboard. And now, for no reason, they'd presented me with an instrument that had the potential to make them pray for profound hearing loss.

Ventriloquism is like audible mime, with words and lame, mean-spirited jokes. My piano recitals were bad enough, but at least you didn't have to pretend to laugh. *Not* laughing was the problem. But now the family would be subjected to daily command performances, their faces frozen in stricken grins as I unleashed hours of borscht-belt groaners through the plastic jaws of my new best friend.

Charlie came with his own case, a blue plastic valise covered with fake painted-on stickers that suggested he'd been quite the world traveler: PARIS, LONDON, BANGKOK. A regular dandy, he was dressed in a tux, bow tie, top hat, and monocle. His face was fixed in an unsettling grimace, the smile of a psychopath, the eyes wide and dead, the ends of his mouth creeping up past his nose in much the same expression that my family made when forced to sit through my routine. A drawstring allowed you to open and close his jaw, chop-chop, like a guillotine.

I was captivated. That this might be uncool did not occur to me; that this could prove a social kiss of death did not register. But of course it was. Being a ventriloquist automatically brands you as a misfit, a loser. No homecoming queen has ever had a cute dummy routine on the side. No big man on campus pulls his crowd-pleasin' little buddy out of his backpack when things get dull in football practice. Sure, every once in a while you'll see it in the talent competition of a pageant, but even then she's the contestant you feel sorry for. Even doing rhythmic gymnastics, even performing "You Light Up My Life" in sign language, is cooler than a dummy act.

But I was delighted and grateful for the distraction. By now I was ten and was starting to become supremely uncomfortable in my body. The entry into double digits had done me in, lighting a fire under my simmering hypochondria. I'd read that your eyesight peaked at ten, and it seemed likely that the rest of my malformed parts were passing their prime as well. Already my joints cracked like popcorn. My pores were getting bigger, and my hair was kinking up. Warts were coming in. My limbs were speckled with dermatitis, and my feet were acquiring ominous cornlike growths. Things were bad, and I knew the gruesome specter of puberty wasn't far off. Our recent Sex Ed unit had confirmed my fears that I was only in for more mortification: acne, body hair, and a host of changes that would invite public comment.

On top of everything else I was suddenly fat. It was really just a matter of time before I turned into a full-blown troll and government forces relocated me to my rightful home under a bridge.

To make matters worse, skinny-dipping had started to become a popular party activity among my friends. I was just mortified. "I think I'll sit this one out," I'd tell the birthday girl as I wandered back into the kitchen to help her mother fix the dip platter. "My doctor doesn't want me to get this rash wet."

But Charlie, like his namesake, could take me away from all that. He was a plastic proxy who could compensate for my insecurities and smooth-talk my way out of any jam. He was, in effect, a body double, and if he couldn't perform my nude scenes for me at least he could say my lines. Charlie was not anatomically correct but anatomically impervious, and could say things that didn't seem appropriate coming out of a pudgy fifth grader. Sure, he was irreverent and sometimes crossed the line, but you couldn't stay mad at him. I imagined the laughs we'd have at parties. "I'd love to join you girls in the pool, but I'm not Scotchgarded," he might say. "I'll just sit this one out and work on my tan."

Only it sounded more like "I'n lun nu noin you nirls in the nool." Charlie had come with an instructional ventriloquism booklet, but actually mastering the technique turned out to be harder than I'd thought. Apparently there was more to it than just speaking through gritted teeth. You had to replace fricatives with convincing soundalikes and write careful scripts to avoid words that contained completely unpronounceable letters like *B* and *P*. Also, it seemed, you had to practice. Soon I was spending hours in front of the bathroom mirror, saying things like "Vell hello, ladies and gerns!" through a clenched jaw.

It was all incredibly annoying, but really, my parents had only themselves to blame. I have no idea what possessed them to buy me the dummy in the first place. I can only guess it was my mother's fondness for Wayland Flowers and Madame, who were frequent guests on *Match Game*, her favorite show.

Some years later, Wayland would die, and it's been reported that the original Madame was buried with him. After a few weeks of my routine, I suspect my parents wanted to do the same to me and Charlie. It was becoming clear that I needed a new audience, so I was beside myself when I saw signs posted for the first-ever Zamora Elementary talent show. Here, finally, was a chance to take my show on the road. If I was lucky, I hoped, there might be a talent scout in the audience, and before long I'd be guesting on the $20,000 *Pyramid* or *Hollywood Squares*.

It took me a couple weeks to get my set down. Progress was slow, impeded by constant fits of cracking myself up. I no longer remember the entire act, but I believe I had some good bits about cafeteria food and tetherball. Because "na-nu na-nu" was easy to say with your mouth closed, there was a lengthy Robin Williams impression. For this reason there was also an extended riff on Naugahyde. "I nean, really. Is it nade of genuine nauga?" I threw in a little political humor about Dresident Jinny Carter and his resemblance to a deanut, and I had my set, a tight fifteen minutes of solid comedy gold.

All that was left was to come up with a costume. I briefly considered dressing as Charlie's twin, but that seemed altogether too lame. A dummy act was one thing, but to dress alike was to invite comparisons, and it was clear which one of us looked better in a tux. Maybe I should go with an old ballet costume? Basic black? Hickish country overalls to contrast with Charlie's uptown polish?

Pictures from the performance reveal that in the end I borrowed a skirt and blouse from my babysitter and pulled my hair back into a bun for a sort of librarian effect. They further reveal that I accessorized with Groucho Marx nose-and-glasses, for reasons I no longer recall and can't begin to guess.

I was the last one to go on. I fidgeted backstage in the library-cum-green-room for what seemed like forever, impatient to get onstage and show everyone how it was done. Just look at these jackasses, this kid doing magic, what a clown. Check out the retard with the flutophone. And here comes Klassic Elegance doing a dance routine to "My Sharona." Please.

Finally I went on. I was *killing.* Oh, good heavens, this was great stuff. It was so good I couldn't stop chuckling, and I kept having to take breaks to pause and compose myself.

I was three minutes into it before I realized I was the only one laughing. It was weirdly quiet, wasn't it? It had been weirdly quiet the whole time.

I tapped at an imaginary mic. "Unnn, ello? Is dis ding on?"

It wasn't that the students were unkind; they were just confused. The first three rows held a hundred kindergartners, all of them baffled, all looking up at me with pure benevolent bewilderment. That was to be expected, maybe, but why did the older kids look so stricken? And what was going on with the parents and teachers? You could tell they were trying—they'd laugh and clap, only at completely arbitrary moments, like right before the big punch line or in the middle of my commercial jingle medley.

It was a disaster. I'd prepared some comebacks in case I got heckled, but what do you do when you get pitied?

Ten minutes later, I was back in the library trying to figure out where I'd gone wrong. Sometime later I would realize that between the Groucho nose and the really crappy ventriloquism, no one could understand a word; it had been ten straight minutes of "ud ih heh tuh tuh nu—enh uh niiiiiigh?" coupled with unintelligible grunting and snorting at my own jokes.

Also, it sort of blew. I definitely should have cut that Mork-from-Ork-in-King-Arthur's-Court bit; it was really too high-concept for K-3. The musical segments were a little flat. The physical comedy was too facile, and my segues could have been tighter.

Worst of all was the fact that I now had two hours of class to get through. I didn't think I'd make it. My classmates had all seen me bomb, and being cooped up with the witnesses was the last thing I wanted. It felt like being trapped in the room in which you'd been farting all day.

"I think I need to go home," I told my mother, who'd come to see me perform.

She lowered her sunglasses and gave me a look. "I think you need to suck it up," she said, and headed for the parking lot. And so I slunk back to my classroom, slumped at my desk, and braced myself for the worst.

It was then that I witnessed the most amazing performance of all: everyone was perfectly nice to me. No one said anything unkind. No one even mentioned it. There were other things to discuss: last night's episode of *Mork and Mindy*, tonight's *Charlie's Angels*. On the way home from school the second-graders didn't heckle me, and at recess, the custodians didn't chuck tomatoes. It was like it had never even happened.

I was shocked, but I shouldn't have been. The truth was that no one ever really said anything cruel to me. That would come later—next year I'd start junior high—but for now, for the most part, my classmates were never anything but nice. I hated my body and the stupid things it did, the scary diseases it might develop, but no one else seemed to notice or care. No

1

one called me fat, or funny-looking, or lame. Those words echoed in my ears all the time, like a chorus, but in fact they were only coming from me, throwing my voice. I was, in a way, a ventriloquist after all, always imagining my self-loathing in others' mouths.

I *was* a really bad ventriloquist, though. "*That* thucked," I told my reflection later that afternoon, gritting my teeth not for technique but in frustration. My career was over. That afternoon I locked Charlie in his case and stashed him in the back of my closet, only bringing him out when the Angels needed a butler. Then I found more interesting activities, like eating disorders, mental illness, cancer scares, and teen angst, and forgot about him altogether.

The next time I'd see him was several years later. My father had followed through on a threat he'd been making for years and rented a Dumpster. I was in junior high by then, and it was high time, my parents said, that we got rid of some of these toys.

So it was that I spent the last week of summer in my stuffy room, rounding up the detritus of childhood, the dolls and stuffed animals and half-broken crap, shoving it all into green plastic bags. I paused when I came across Charlie. "What do I do with this? It was so expensive, it seems wrong to just throw it out."

My mother held a bag already half full of naked Angel dolls. "Eh," she said, holding the bag out to me. "Who needs it. Come on. Dump the body."

Who needs it. Maybe she was right. By then my own body

had changed, and not at all in the ways I was expecting. My brain had short-circuited and I'd developed an eating disorder that both solved the fat issue and effectively delayed puberty. I was too busy figuring out how many calories were in a breath mint to worry about the carcinogens in the neighborhood, and my hypochondria settled down too. The food issue was a much bigger problem, of course, but it was true: I didn't need Charlie anymore, and though it made me sad to do it, I stuffed him in the bag.

It was sort of sad, reuniting with old friends only to chuck them out. I was an overdramatic child, tending to read poetic symbolism into the most mundane activities—a simple trip to the post office became an allegory for the human spirit taking wing—but it was hard not to view this as anything but a symbolic scene, a one-act play about the end of childish things.

Many years later I'd realize that it was actually a scene about failing to appreciate. And while it's true that I failed to appreciate the important things, like a body that, though imperfect, is basically healthy, and a brain that, though hypochondriac, is generally functional, I mean "appreciate" in a purely financial sense. If we'd held on to even a small fraction of what was thrown out that day, all now worth substantial sums, none of us would have to work. I go on eBay and just cringe. My mother was right about the Charlie doll—you can pick one of those up for under thirty dollars—but the rest of it turned out to be worth a lot. Had we filled the Dumpster with gold bullion we could not have thrown out more money. The style-your-own Farrah head, the Kate Jackson dolls, the hundreds of *Charlie's*

Angels baseball cards, the Donny and Marie paraphernalia, the *Dukes of Hazzard* lunch box, the *Peanuts* collectibles—those turned out to be the things of real value. And at night, when I can't sleep, I picture Charlie lying in the landfill, surrounded by miniature Kate Jacksons and Jaclyn Smiths, Cheryl Ladds and Shelley Hacks. Through gritted teeth he's chuckling at our stupidity: Vut dunnies you turned out to de. And he is, as always, correct.

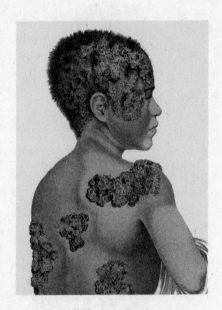

Fig. 4. Tinea Favosa

5.

Conversion Disorder

❁

I f you're Catholic, you start confessing around the time of
your first communion, but the rest of us generally begin at
puberty. I was twelve and there was something I had to tell my
parents. I didn't know if I could do it. My classmates had to
confess things like "I got my period," or "I'm pretty sure I'm
gay," or "I've decided to become a vegan." And these are all
difficult admissions, to be sure, but any parent could accept
them, move on, heal. I was going to have to tell my parents I
had breast cancer.

I'd noticed the mass a week or two before, and it was taking
me a while to work up the nerve. Breast cancer was so much
more embarrassing than melanoma or muscular dystrophy.
And it was so serious, so sad. I hated to break the bad news.
Plus, it was coming at such a bad time. I was too busy to get
fatally ill. I'd just wrapped up that yearlong foray into anorexia,
followed by a bang-up bout of OCD that had resulted in a spectacular antibacterial breakdown. I barely had that under some

sort of control and now my bat mitzvah was just a month away. Oh, and since it was my father and not my mother who was Jewish, I was going to have to convert first. Things were a little hectic.

It was all so overwhelming, the cancer and the conversion and the million things left to do. I woke up every day under a cloud of dread. It wasn't that I had doubts about making my faith official. Judaism was a natural match for my neuroses. The conversion felt like getting a sex change operation: I already knew I was Jewish on the inside, and now we just needed to make my external reality match.

Like a sex change, however, this was going to require nudity, and that, of course, was the part that was getting me worked up. The conversion demanded a visit to the mikvah, the ritual bath, and witnesses would have to be present to ensure I did everything properly.

Though the Internet might lead you to believe differently, pubescent girls don't really like to take their clothes off in front of other people, and I liked it less than most. Gym was bad enough, but at least you could leave your underpants on, and the girls with stomach hickeys drew almost all the attention, anyway. But in the mikvah you'd have to be witnessed. That was the point.

For the budding hypochondriac, puberty is a piñata filled with mysterious and awful new ways to get sick. Suddenly you have all these new parts to get infected. And they're such *meaningful* parts, such troubling and emotionally fraught appendages. It's very common for hypochondriacs to obsess over their genitals, which seems fitting considering the disease's reputation as a form of mental masturbation. There are, in fact, several hypochondriacal syndromes that focus exclusively on fear of semen loss (*dhat* and *jiryan* in India; *sukra prameha* in Sri Lanka, and *shenkui* in China and Thailand). In a hypochondriacal condition called *koro*, found in parts of South Asia and Africa, sufferers become convinced that their breasts or genitals are retracting. Believing that they'll die when the things finally disappear, panic ensues. To forestall death the male sufferer will clamp his penis into a wooden box or tie it to a peg. He might choose to hold on to it instead, or ask his wife or a friend to. In spite or perhaps because of this, epidemics occasionally occur. A few years ago one swept through Sudan when residents became convinced Zionists were trying to kill them with "penis-melting cyborg combs." It reached such a fever pitch the minister of health had to issue statements to put their fears to rest.

All the Zionists were going to do to me was make me take a bath, but that was bad enough. It didn't help much that I'd known it was coming. I'd been studying for my conversion for a year, and if I'd learned anything about Judaism it was that it monitored the body, everything it does, all that goes in or comes out of it. The Talmud is full of bodily restrictions and medical guidelines. Many of the rabbis who wrote it were, in fact, physicians. Judaism has linked the two roles since Biblical times, when the priests did the diagnosing and treating. You think you're embarrassed to go to a doctor with a wart down there; imagine having to take it to your minister.

The most famous Jewish scholar, Maimonides, was the private physician to the sultan of Egypt, and was considered a leading medical authority of the Middle Ages. Somewhat predictably for a Jewish doctor, his medical advice trumpets the curative powers of chicken soup, noting that it helps restore proper balance of the humors, especially black bile, the supposed cause of hypochondria. Less predictably, he comments that chicken testicles are full of nutrients and are especially good for the sick and weak. (He goes on to say that, really, any animal's testicles have many restorative properties.) For asthma, he prescribes what is essentially a chicken-soup enema (chicken fat with oil, juice, and herbs).

The Talmud is full of the doctor-rabbis' recommendations and rules, and they leave no gallstone unturned. Physicians are required to examine, and examine closely; diagnosis can take up to three weeks. You're explicitly instructed to see specialists whenever possible. You're told not to live in a town without a doctor or, more oddly, vegetable gardens. You can't eat food you've stored under your bed. Uncovered water is off-limits because snakes might have gotten into it; imperfect fruit is banned for the same reason. Nothing is left unregulated. The Talmud even enumerates all the different kinds of genital discharge, and tells you what to do when you have one.

The Talmud tells you what to wash, wear, eat, wash, wash,

wash. Trust us: you want to wash. Well before the microscope was invented, the rabbis knew there was something to fear, even if they couldn't see it yet: ". . . there are many germs and insects that are dangerous to health; minute organisms existing everywhere in abundance; if man could see them all, he could not exist."

As a clinical handbook the Talmud is sort of interesting. The Talmud's grasp of medicine, current at the time, now strikes readers as a little odd. The rabbis prescribe drinking urine (aged forty days, to reverse snake poison; fresh donkey's, to treat jaundice) a little more than doctors do nowadays, and they're terrified of sweat. Sweat was considered so dangerous, the rabbis said you couldn't touch any potentially sweaty part of the body during a meal, or hold bread under your arm. Some of the precautions seem extreme, but still, if you've ever seen a pizza maker stick a ball of dough in his bare armpit while he answers the phone—as the employees of my local pizza joint sometimes do—the Talmud strikes you as perfectly reasonable.

Interestingly, the Talmud never mentions hypochondria. It's like the old saw about Chinese food just being food in China. In Judaism, hypochondria is just being practical.

Guilt and blame, however, are there in spades. The Talmud explicitly links physical health and spiritual health. It's a simple conversion: sin leads straight to disease. Gossip and you can expect leprosy; forget to light your Sabbath candles and say hello to infertility. If you're sick, you probably deserve it.

Of all the things hypochondriacs fear, this is the idea we fear the most. Nothing is scarier than the disease we think we've brought on ourselves. For that reason, of course, genital conditions rate high in the hypochondriac imagination. So do conditions that seem symbolic or mythical: going deaf if you think you're a bad listener, or blind if you masturbate a lot.

There's a specific form of hypochondria called conversion disorder whose sufferers do just that. They become blind or deaf or lame for no physical reason at all. There's usually a pretty good emotional one, though. The woman who finds herself hamstrung by her divorce is suddenly unable to walk; the teenager prone to blind rage suddenly can't see. Doctors don't know why or how it happens, and tests turn up nothing.

The hallmark of conversion disorder is something called *la belle indifference*—a complete lack of concern with the troubling symptom. Most patients would be panic-stricken if they suddenly went deaf, but patients with conversion disorder seem at most mildly amused. Although psychiatric diagnostic manuals don't note it, *la belle indifference* is also a symptom of adolescence, medicalese for "whatever." It is the impulse that makes you roll your eyes at your parents, pretend to hate the things you love, become a vegan, accept a hand job from your bunkmate at camp, or lock yourself in your room for six years and write bad nihilistic poetry.

I was thirteen; "whatever" was my wheelhouse. But I didn't have conversion disorder. I'm just not that good. I can translate anxiety into a pinkish eye, but I can't actually get it to go blind. I could convert worry over my conversion to Judaism and adulthood into panic over a lumpy mass, but that was about it.

There *were* any number of reasons I deserved breast cancer, though. My reading material alone was enough. In the past year alone, I'd inhaled *Forever*, *The Clan of the Cave Bear* (filthy), and *The Valley of the Horses* (even worse). I wasn't particularly obsessed with my own genitals, but I'd found Ayla's and Jondalar's pretty interesting. What rabbi was going to wave me in once he found out how well-read I was on that? And he *would* find out. I had breast cancer, after all, and probably leprosy too. It was all right there in the Talmud.

Catholics seem positively laid-back in comparison. I'm no expert in theology, but Catholicism, it seems to me, is a religion based on the philosophy of the makeover, with its emphasis on resurrection of the flesh and transubstantiation, of water into wine, of sins washed clean by confession. The host itself may be the best example: bread recast as body.

Catholicism grants you do-overs. Perhaps this is why my mother is never particularly disturbed by the body, even at its worst. This is a woman who's given sponge baths to hospice patients, who, without vomiting, wrestles the slimy ten-year-old clump of hair that's backing up the shower, who took charge when the dog became aroused and, well, "took out his lipstick." When the cat eats every part of the mouse except its butt, leaving it as an offering for her to step in, she does not blink. As a young woman she once went to an autopsy—on a *date*—an experience she would later recommend to her own children. "They pull the whole face off, and crack the ribs. It's something you never forget."

It is this lack of squeamishness that allows her to serve as a eucharistic minister, even after she was bitten by a parishioner. (This, I'll admit, she brought on herself. She'd given the host to a dozy senior, then stuck her finger in the lady's mouth to fish it out, worried that she'd choke. The woman promptly came to and chomped down.)

My mother did not sue. And here we arrive at the critical difference between Catholicism and Judaism. If Catholicism views the body as bionic, Judaism views it as a particularly fragile tchotchke; you break it, you buy it. And you will break it. Perhaps because of the Jewish gene pool and cultural tendency toward hypochondria, the Jewish view of the body tends to be fairly pessimistic. Ear hair, monobrows, stubby legs, frizz—so much has gone wrong already, anything could happen next. It seems a cruel but fitting irony that the Hebrew word for body is *goof.*

In the Talmud, the body is called the *kil,* the vessel, a piece of earthenware. The implication is that the body and soul are not at all one; the body is only a temporary address, and this is the only comfort. It might be a dump, but you're just renting.

With my conversion I'd be changing landlords. Hence, the mikvah: the vessel had to be immersed. It was just like washing dishes. This was something I'd done obsessively for the past year, and when I thought of it that way, it wasn't so hard.

I plunged in, charged forward, mumbled a blessing, and jumped out. It was over in a flash.

IN TRADITIONAL JUDAISM, the last-ditch treatment for serious illness is to change the sufferer's name. The idea is that the angel of death will get confused and leave without his prey. He's come to claim Izzy Epstein, not Ira, but there appears to be no Izzy at this address, so let's just get some lunch and call it a day.

The other time you take a new name is when you convert. I chose poorly—my Hebrew name, it turns out, is a homonym for one of the genital discharges the Talmud mentions. Still, it could do the trick. There's no Jennifer Traig here, but Vaginal Pus Traig is alive and well.

She was. About a week after the conversion I worked up my nerve and told my parents about the tumor. An exam was performed—shirtless, so just in case I didn't have a tumor I could still die from embarrassment.

The results confirmed that I did not have breast cancer. What I had were breasts, and this was just as bad. Puberty had begun, and with it all those new ways to die: ectopic pregnancies and ovarian tumors, cysts of all kinds and toxic shock.

I did not know, yet, that this, too, was a false alarm, a symptom that would go no further. Thanks to nutritional deficiencies caused by the other things that had been keeping me so busy at the time—the anorexia and the obsessive-compulsive weirdness with food—puberty was still several years off. Well, most of it, anyway. *La belle indifference* was already here.

"I'm not dying, then?" I asked my parents, when I'd gotten the all clear. "Whatever. I didn't really think I was. I can't believe you actually looked worried there. Yeesh. You two need to relax."

I folded my arms across my chest, grabbed *The Clan of the Cave Bear* and my notebooks, stomped up to my room, and slammed the door. I had some bad nihilistic poetry to write, and I didn't want to be disturbed.

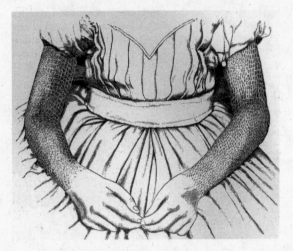

Fig. 5. Ichthyosis, or Fish-Skin Disease

6.

Socialized Medicine

❁

The first time I gave all my friends diarrhea was in high school, but I'd go on to do it again and again. Due to a complete lack of kitchen skills and a tendency to serve things on the tartare side, it happens fairly often. Usually there's more than one suspect dish in each meal, making it hard to pin down the offender, a situation that can lead to repeat infections when you mistakenly decide the deviled eggs were responsible but the spinach dip should still be fine. The only thing I've learned is to be honest with my guests; now, they eat at their own risk. "I'm not going to lie to you," I say as I take their coats. "The tuna sat out for four hours yesterday, and I'm pretty sure I saw the cat stick a paw in it. I think it's fine, but you never know."

You never know. It's a strange thing, food poisoning. It's one of the fastest ways for a healthy person to get terribly sick. It's not at all uncommon, and will happen to most people several times in their lives, more often if they attend parties at my house. Most of the time it will be fairly mild, but it can be serious or even fatal. There are even law firms that specialize in it, though you hate to imagine what sorts of specimens are entered into evidence.

Still, the lawsuits seem justified; because it so often comes from dining out, it's one of the only sicknesses you actually pay to acquire, and it can in fact be very dangerous. It can cause nerve damage and rheumatoid arthritis, doing permanent harm to body parts you wouldn't expect it to affect. I have a friend who still can't feel her thumb thanks to some bad piroshki she ate seven years ago. Outbreaks of rye poisoning in fourteenth-century England caused sufferers to bark like dogs, see demons, and—yeesh—hemorrhage vaginally.

Still, it's my favorite way to be ill. Hypochondria can be terribly lonely, but food poisoning is a party. It's just such a *social* way to get sick. It's communal. You share some food with friends, and some sadistic microorganisms, and then you all get horribly sick and it's awful but you're all in this together. For the hypochondriac, it's like a busman's holiday. And you're *really* sick! You're not imagining things! You're sharing this powerful experience, a fleeting but profoundly moving event that that makes you appreciate things you normally take for granted, like continence.

Food poisoning has a long and proud history. It is, in a way, part of our genesis myth: Adam and Eve stumble upon a bad apple, and everything follows from there. Food poisoning is as old as food is, and it's played an important role throughout history. The Athenians' loss of the Peloponnesian War was due, in part, to spoiled cereal. It's been theorized that the

Salem witch trials were brought on by widespread hallucinations caused by food poisoning from a rye fungus (LSD, in fact, is derived from it). It even factors in theology. Buddha's death was due to bad pork, and food poisoning shows up in the Bible, when a bunch of Israelites perish after getting ahold of some bad quail.

The culprit in that case was probably something called coturnism, which is just one of hundreds of food-borne illnesses that can cause terrible, terrible poisoning. There's listeria and salmonella, shigella and botulism. It can be bacteria or a virus, a protozoan or a parasite, a lodger checking into your gastrointestinal motel for a few days or so.

They are bad guests. Microorganisms are the visitors who poop in the communal ice machine. Food poisoning is, literally, a shitty sickness, often caused by fecal-oral transmission. Even if you, like me, retain a habit of neurotic handwashing, crap can creep in one way or another. Maybe a pet will be responsible, or maybe fertilizer will. There are lots of ways to get sick.

In the Catholic Church, where "host" means something else entirely, they've changed the way they administer the wafer in the last few years for that very reason. Sure, the eucharistic minister is probably a good washer, but you never know where the rest of the congregation has been, and some of them, of course, bite. Letting a stranger stick their hand in your mouth after they've done the same thing to a hundred or so other people—including, at my best friend's parish, the woman who wears a sleeping bag that by all appearances does double duty as her bidet—no longer seems like such a good idea, and now, you're often handed the wafer to put in your mouth yourself.

As a Jew, I was spared these dangers, but being Jewish posed its own set of hazards, Jewish summer camp the most hazardous of all. I don't know what happens at, say, Catholic camp—given their access to self-flagellants and exorcism supplies, I imagine it's actually worse—but the difference is they're prepared for it, trained by years of kneeling and penitence and the belief in resurrection. For Jews, however, camp is a minefield of foreign perils: underheated pools and mosquitoes, pollen, processed industrial foods, hiking, and communal bathrooms. Worse than that, of course, was no bathroom at all. The need for indoor plumbing is common to all Jews. For this reason the overnight hikes were widely dreaded, and routinely ended with a troupe of constipated preteens uncomfortably shuffling their way back to camp.

My own Jewish summer camp was, as camps go, only semi-tough. Stridently Zionist in theory, it was much more lax in practice, favored by young intellectuals who spent most of their time in the lodge discussing Hannah Arendt. The most strenuous things we had to endure were lectures on the glories of Socialism. Sure, it was stricter than the marshmallowy Reform camps—which allowed, for instance, marshmallows, unkosher contraband here—but there were tougher. The most hard-core were a sort of scout troupe founded by Israeli expatriates who were afraid their American-raised children would grow up too soft. According to my friends who were lucky enough to join, they trained on actual guns and practiced defending themselves against guerrilla warfare. At retreats they were regularly woken in the middle of the night by shouts of "*Azaka! Azaka!*"—Attack! Attack!—a defensive drill that sent suburban kids tearing down the tree-lined streets of Palo Alto, curly-haired commandos in Lacoste shirts and Esprit jeans.

Our group was less demanding but it was not without its physical hazards, most of them in the cafeteria. One summer, the kitchen was run by a taciturn skinhead we later learned was a prodigious alcoholic who was drunk all summer, though the square falafel should have tipped us off. Meals were presented without beverages or serving spoons, a situation that quickly degenerated into mealtime at the monkey house, as dehydrated campers dipped into the communal serving dishes with their own forks and hands. By the second week of camp, everyone was sick, and the infirmary had run through the entire summer's supply of cold medicine. This was Socialism: we shared everything, even viruses.

Because they were allowed to come for free the camp was popular with recent Russian immigrants. The Russian kids, who knew firsthand what Socialism actually meant, were smart enough to bring their own food. Thanks to an Eastern European philosophy of food preservation, however, they also brought their own microorganisms, and I will never forget how, on day five, the salamis stashed in their duffel bags went off like an alarm.

"I don't know how you do things in the Soviet Union, but

here in America we don't keep meat with our underpants," we told them. "The whole point of you being at this camp is to get socialized in the ways of your new country, and that's just not going to happen as long as you hide sausage under your bed."

Even when you don't pack your own rotting food, camp can be a great place to get food poisoning. One of the more common protozoa is, in fact, called campylobacter. It's often called by its nickname, "campy," which conjures images of drag queens stumbling through the woods. The name turns out to be only an etymologic coincidence—campylobacter is simply Greek for "bent bacteria"—but all the same, a fitting one.

Because I hate camping, I generally limited my trips to overnight retreats, which was the longest I could go without a bathroom. In spite of this, I was promoted to counselor when I turned eighteen and promptly assumed leadership of the local troupe. Except for the folk songs, it was not disagreeable: there was a small stipend and not a lot of work, and the kids were mostly the well-behaved offspring of my professors. Every few weeks or so we gathered for puppet shows on the history of the Balfour Declaration, and a couple of times a year we hunkered down for a weekend-long retreat.

These tended to be low-budget affairs where you were invited to imagine some nearby swampland as the Galilee, your brusque American counselors as brusque native Israelis. On the weekend retreat I remember best we'd gathered in an empty elementary school we were imagining as a kibbutz for a traditional Zionist Shabbat. This consisted mostly of singing

Hebrew folk songs and playing Ga Ga, a game I didn't understand and did not care to, as it seemed to involve physical exer-
tion. I was far more interested in the alternate Israeli activities
of drinking instant coffee and ordering the kids around. It was
like normal life, only everything had a Hebrew name. Instead
of counselors we had *madrichim*; instead of spirit, *ruach*; instead of Nescafé, *cafe nes*, which the *madrichim* drank in the
mizbeach while ignoring the *yeladim*.

Instead of social action we had *tikkun olam*, which was the
part I dreaded, as it tended to involve far more effort than
drinking *cafe nes*. On Saturday we would learn all about the
oppressed Jews of the Soviet Union, and on Sunday, we'd do
something about it. We'd chartered a bus to drive us to the
Soviet consulate, where, filled with socialist Zionist *ruach* and
yet more *cafe nes*, we were going to stage a protest.

At the time, Soviet Jewry was a popular cause with America's Jewish preteens. It was de rigueur to have a twin bar mitzvah, chanting your Torah portion in honor of the little Soviet
Jew who could not have a bar mitzvah of his own. You'd exchange letters and pictures and bask in the satisfaction of sharing your mitzvah with little Oleg. Sure, he didn't get your Atari
or your savings bonds, but he did get some wallet-size photos
of you in your prayer shawl and oversize yarmulke. From each
according to his ability, to each according to his needs.

That alone should have been enough. Helping them once
they got to this country by inviting them to free summer
camps and politely ignoring their rotting sausages should have
been enough. But we were tireless, so we were also willing, on

the weekend in question, to spend a Sunday morning holding up some signs in front of the Soviet consulate while we worked on our tans.

It was late on Saturday night when it became apparent something was wrong. The head counselor pulled me aside as I made my way to my sleeping bag on the cafeteria floor. "You didn't eat any mayonnaise, did you?" she whispered.

"Yes, I ate the mayonnaise," I whined. "Lunch was egg salad, tuna salad, potato salad, and coleslaw. I'm pretty sure even the *Danish* had mayonnaise in it. We all ate the mayonnaise. Why?"

"There might be a—oh, just— Never mind. I'm sure it'll be fine."

True food poisoning has an incubation period of twelve to thirty-six hours. Twenty-four is fairly average. And so it was precisely when we arrived at the Soviet consulate the next morning that the salmonella kicked in.

For the first fifteen minutes or so we could pretend it was nothing. Food poisoning is, in many ways, the inverse of hypochondria. Hypochondriacs pretend they're sick; food poisoning victims pretend they're not. It was just the bumpy bus ride, you tell yourself, or too many cups of *cafe nes*, but surely not this, surely this will pass. We were Zionists given to poring over maps of Mesopotamia. If denial was anything other than a river in Egypt, we wouldn't have known.

But the specter of a couple dozen vomiting Jews was hard to ignore, and it quickly became apparent that we were all very, very sick. The younger kids were the first to go: the nine-year-olds meekly asking for plastic bags before vomiting down their shirts, then the tweens, looking helplessly for a trash can. The high school students went next, bringing the counselors down with them.

At first we tried to vomit discreetly in the consulate's bushes, but that didn't last long. As the protozoa escalated their assault we simply lay where we landed on the sidewalk. It was quite a spectacle: twenty-odd campers and counselors curled like shofars around puddles of our own sick with protest signs at our sides. Every once in a while someone would lift his head and mumble, "Free the Soviet Jews!" but mostly this was drowned out by the retching.

The old Russian term for food poisoning, *zlaia korcha,* means "evil writhing," and that's exactly what this was. But it was also, somehow, redemptive. At the time, Soviet Jews were known as refuseniks, so it seemed only appropriate, our protest, launching refuse on the consulate lawn. I half-wondered if it had been planned. More recently that very thing has become a favorite technique of antiwar activists, who drink red, white, and blue milk, then vomit the flag to say the war makes them sick. We vomited orange juice and bagels, but still, it made a statement.

Less than a year later, the Soviet Union eased its restrictions on Jews, and record numbers were allowed to emigrate. I'm sure it had to do with larger forces—the fall of Communism, the rise of perestroika and glasnost, global pressure on Russia to improve its stance on human rights—but I couldn't help thinking we had something to do with it. "The land will vomit you out," reads a Torah passage we'd studied in one of our youth group sessions. It's about ejecting apostate Jews from Canaan, not secular Jews from Kiev, but at the time the prophecy seemed true enough.

In our lectures on Socialism, we never learned about social-ization, about the ways we're shaped by forces like culture, or illness, and the way illness shapes society in turn. But of course it does. Food poisoning is especially influential, leading to lost wars and murderous hysteria. Even imagined illness can have an impact; hypochondria, after all, was one of the guiding aes-thetics of the eighteenth and nineteenth centuries.

There was never too much hypochondria in the Soviet Union. Imaginary illness just didn't get you out of work. Ma-lingering, however, did, and Soviet citizens got very adept at faking fevers by rubbing mustard and peppers in their armpits before doctor visits. This also provided a nice garnish for the luncheon meat you might have stored in your undershorts.

The practice of using fake symptoms to shirk work was widespread, and I sometimes wonder if the consulate employ-ees, peering at us behind drawn curtains, thought we were just faking like their comrades. Maybe they thought it was a crazy Zionist plot, or maybe they chalked it up to *zlaia korcha* or some bad salami. What did it matter? A year later, the Soviet Union was no more, and Soviet Jews could do as they wished. We'd won.

But food poisoning leaves a funny taste in your mouth, and, as it turns out, this did too. The Soviet Jews left the Soviet Union, but things didn't go as well as we'd hoped. The adjustment to their new homes in the United States proved somewhat rocky; their socialization, incomplete. They were depressed, unemployed, they didn't fit in.

Studies were done on the new immigrants, and the results revealed unusually high levels of hypochondria. They had developed all kinds of unpleasant symptoms, which required all kinds of treatments and tests. Only now they were in a country without socialized medicine. It was the least we could do.

Fig. 6. Molluscum Fibrosum

7.

Occupational Therapy

Except for the occasional bouts of food poisoning and the psychiatric problems, my teen years were fairly comfortable. Then the day after I graduated from high school my parents decided to ruin my life and make me get a job. I really hadn't seen this coming. For the previous few years I'd been disabled by the aforementioned anorexia and OCD, and I'd thought that being crazy would exempt me from this sort of thing; that was one of its perks. But now that I was better my parents thought I should work. I'd recovered from my eating disorder, and it was time to start pulling my weight.

"The gravy train has derailed," my mother announced. "You are getting a j-o-b. I don't care if you cap bottles, operate the Tilt-A-Whirl, or sell your own plasma, but for twenty hours a week you're going to be someone else's problem and they're going to pay you for the privilege."

This was my cue to cover my ears and sing over the disturbing talk-talk. "La-la-la," I sang, "Ku-ku-ru-ku, no can hear you. I can't help it, la-la, there's a choir in my head. The angels are singing a psa-ah-ah-alm about liquid hand soap, soap-soap-soap!"

I was hoping she'd think I'd relapsed and relent. A job. Geez. It didn't seem fair. It wasn't that I hadn't been *working*. It was that I hadn't been getting *paid*. But I'd been working for years, dieting and worrying about my health and performing my various compulsions, and I thought I deserved a little vacation before I started college.

But my parents didn't see it that way, and even my sister was unsympathetic. She'd been working since the day she'd turned sixteen, making and occasionally fouling pizzas at an upscale eatery I knew better than to dine at. For her, work was not an obligation but an escape. Even though it lacked a deep fryer, this restaurant was widely regarded by our classmates as the best place to work. The food was good, and the supervision was light. Vicky sometimes passed out in a booth when she was supposed to be cleaning, and once, she'd baked a large pink plastic hoop earring into a pizza. She'd had to clamp a hand over her other ear when the lucky recipient brought it to the counter, but even then she didn't get fired. High jinks happened. I'd heard the staff sometimes turned the kitchen into a giant Cuisinart by throwing balls of dough into the ceiling fan, and when the seven-foot-long plastic phone fell off the top of the delivery van, they'd amused themselves for hours pretending to make calls on it. They also seemed to be a little lax with the tap. I pictured Vicky's working life as a movie, a teen romp with Bill Murray playing the boss, leading his army of shiny young kitchen staff in an insurrection against the stuffed shirt of an owner.

Vicky worked as many hours as my parents would permit. She'd come home reeking of tomato paste and yeast, her face flushed with the satisfaction of a job well done, cash in her pocket, and, I suspected, a little sampling of the tap. I think it embarrassed her that my only significant work experience was caring for the neighbor's plants when they went out of town.

"Don't you want more of a résumé builder than 'watered pansies'?" she'd ask. "Isn't that, like, the résumé for *rain*?"

When it became clear I was going to do exactly nothing to find a job myself, my father caved and arranged one for me at the clinic where he practiced. I'm sure it killed him to do this. It was embarrassing, asking for a favor like this, suggesting that you thought you were entitled to such things, and that your daughter would be needing your help for a long, long time.

Because I could type, the favor was granted—somewhat begrudgingly, I gathered—and now I was stuck. My father had humbled himself for me, and there was no way I was getting out of this. They were really going to make me do it.

What bothered me was *why*. There was some talk of saving up some money for college, but at $4.25 an hour, I was barely earning enough to pay for my diet sodas. Besides, I was going to a state school. We all knew the real reason they were making me do this was to get me out of the house.

"It'll be good for you," my mother said. "You'll learn all about the working world, and I bet you'll have fun. You can go on breaks, drink coffee with your co-workers, talk about your soap operas."

"Have you met me?"

"It's for two damn months. Suck it up."

The other advantage of this job was that it was in the same complex as my psychologist's office, so should I have a complete work-induced meltdown, the person who was authorized to fire the tranquilizer dart was only a few steps away.

A work-induced meltdown seemed entirely possible. Couldn't they see that a medical office was the *worst* place for me to be? I was an obsessive-compulsive hypochondriac. It was like hiring a bulimic to run the corn dog cart. In the *bathroom*.

Hypochondria among health professionals is so prevalent, in fact, that it's been classified as its own phenomenon: "Medical school syndrome." When you're learning about the million things that can kill you, it's not uncommon to think you have one or two, and many budding doctors and nurses suffer such situational hypochondria. It almost always passes. Still, it's not all that unusual to see doctors and nurses hooking themselves up to EKGs and blood pressure cuffs when things get slow. The world's most famous nurse, Florence Nightingale, was a prodigious hypochondriac. It's been theorized that she was really sick with a tropical infectious disease, and that's possible, but it's certain she was a terrible hysteric. She took to her bed in 1857, convinced she was at death's door. There she stayed for the next fifty-three years, finally succumbing at age ninety.

But even Florence Nightingale had worked, propped up on her pillows, designing hospitals and drafting plans. My office wasn't going to be as comfortable. I'd be working in medical records. The clinic was switching over to a new computerized system that required all patients to have a blue plastic ID card with their name and a newly assigned patient number, and it was my job to produce them. These were made on an industrial typewriter capable of typing on card blanks. Every forty minutes the machine would overheat and start shuddering violently, then belch out smoke and a strange petrochemical odor. This was my cue to sit and do nothing for ten minutes. By then I'd need a break too, as the typing required more upper-body strength than I'd expected. The keys had to be struck with force, producing a clacking so loud it surprised me I wasn't relegated to work in a distant office, or the parking lot.

I was more or less in the bowels as it was. The clinic was a pleasant 1970s complex of terrariums, ferns, and wood paneling, but the medical records office was in the basement, a low-ceilinged fluorescent-lit dungeon of shelves and gray steel, managed by a steely matriarch with a gray beehive whose sassy but good-hearted demeanor reminded me of the waitresses on *Alice*. Because I was shy, and because the noise of the typewriter prohibited it, I rarely spoke with my co-workers, but they struck me as kind and inoffensive. They were all unmarried women, spinsters, divorcées, the newly engaged, and they were quick to share snacks and makeup tips.

My hours were from nine o'clock until one o'clock. It only took a couple days for me to develop a routine. Every morning I left my house at five to nine and walked the two blocks to the clinic, the day already sticky-hot. At eleven o'clock I took my break, and sat doing nothing in front of the terrarium for fifteen minutes. At one o'clock I turned off my sizzling typewriter, and by five after one I'd be home again. I'd eat the same lunch of pineapple cottage cheese and two of those Stella D'Oro biscuits that are popular with diabetics. Most days I'd spend the rest of the afternoon reading Jane Austen novels and writing out my schedule for the following day: 8:55: Leave for work. 11:00: Take break. 1:05: Get home. 1:10: Eat pineapple cottage cheese and two Stella D'Oro biscuits. 1:30: Write schedule.

Twice a week I was scheduled to walk back to the clinic after lunch to see my psychologist. I showed up as expected, but as the summer wore on these sessions felt more and more perfunctory. They were redundant. I was doing well, and as much as I hated to admit it, I suspected this had something to do with my job. Oh, I still had my obsessive-compulsive habits—I always washed my hands after touching the medical records, and I could not bring myself to type names that contained any religious reference—but on the whole I was doing just fine. I didn't worry about catching the diseases documented in the records all around me. I could do my work and interact with my co-workers, and when I had a troubling thought I could usually manage to let it go. I sometimes wondered if anyone noticed the stack of medical records that was accumulating in my to-do tray, the Godfreys and Gaylords, the Christophers and Christinas, but I didn't obsess about it.

The job was becoming a kind of therapy in itself. I was

surprised to find that except for the noise, I didn't mind it at all; I liked having somewhere to go, something to do. It was the kind of busywork position people take while in rehab, repetitive and physical, a Zen exercise, and it suited me. The work was satisfying and methodical. It was a pleasing business of assigning numbers to people. You could reduce an entire medical history, all the messy fistulae and infections and tumors with teeth and hair, to a seven-digit number on a blue plastic card.

That, I suppose, is what I like about medical work—imposing order on the chaos of our bodies. It's even a job title: orderly. For a hypochondriac, always in fear of the body's unpredictability, it's tremendously satisfying. Fall came and I went off to college as scheduled, but there were breaks and then there was graduation, and I found myself returning to medical offices again and again. I've worked in hospitals and health agencies over half my life. I've done just about everything you can do without actually touching anyone: credential doctors, wrangle Medicare recipients, field complaints, enroll patients, monitor blood, track cadavers.

In occupational therapy, the real kind, patients learn to work with disabilities that initially seemed crippling. And having an occupation, having that first job, did exactly that. It made sickness less scary, cancer boring, GI disasters routine. Like true occupational therapy, it taught me that self-sufficiency is curative, and that there's a value in keeping busy.

But more important, it taught me the value of *looking* busy.

This is the other great advantage of working in a hospital: no other workplace offers so many places to lie down. Motorized beds, exam tables, gurneys—everywhere you look, there's an inviting place to sleep. And there's nothing more curative than a nap you're getting an hourly wage to take.

Fig. 7. Lupus Erythematosus

8.

Textbook Case

✣

F ull-blown hypochondria normally begins around young
adulthood. Mine, a textbook case, came into its own in
college. Freshman-year dizzy spells gave way to shortness of
breath, difficulty swallowing, and mysterious headaches, and
it wasn't long before I was asking for blood work and throat
cultures. I was in school: it only seemed right that I'd be taking tests.

Adult hypochondria is significantly different from the pediatric form. Children generally aren't true hypochondriacs, at
least in a strict clinical sense. All children exhibit hypochondriac behavior, of course, asking for a Band-Aid when their
feelings are hurt, insisting they need to stay in bed when they
dread an assignment. Children aren't adept at articulating
emotions, and it's common for them to translate unhappiness
into physical pain. "I have a stomachache" usually just means
"The fact that you served tuna casserole for dinner proves you
really don't love me." For adults it's more complicated, and
many other factors come into play. Children are hypochondri-

acs to get attention. Adults are hypochondriacs to get attention and drugs.

It's hard to say which I liked better, but college provided plenty of both. The combination of free time, fully covered medical services, and an eye for details was deadly. Every bump and bug bite sent me scurrying to the medical section of the library and then to Student Health Services.

I liked to think I was keeping things interesting. Hypochondria is the variety pack of diseases, ideal for someone who can't commit to lupus or lymphoma. There are, of course, the single-minded sufferers, who spend their entire lives convinced they have one disease in particular, but many of us flit from one to the next. I myself am partial to most cancers and degenerative neurological conditions, but every once in a while I like to mix it up with bone disease or pulmonary failure. My father had worked at the university hospital as a medical student and complained that he saw nothing but mono and tonsillitis. Surely his successors were amused by my Guillain-Barré syndrome and beriberi, my buboes and flesh-eating bacteria?

College is, in fact, a pretty good place to get sick. Besides free medical care, there are all kinds of bugs around. I avoided "dorm disease"—meningitis—but I did get the clichéd case of mono, some strep throat here, pinkeye there. These things get around on a campus. So do the noncontagious time bombs that might be lurking in your DNA. College is the time all sorts of terrifying diseases first present themselves: bipolar disorder and schizophrenia, Hodgkin's and Crohn's.

College is also a ripe time for developing an eating disorder.

That first year of college I was fully over mine, which was even worse. When you're a recently recovered anorexic, the freshman fifteen are as bad as lung cancer—worse, since cancer generally makes you lose weight.

Once again I felt supremely uncomfortable in my body. And this contributed to the hypochondria, too: it was easier to blame a suspected glandular condition than my habit of buttering pizza. Maybe it was diabetes, or a sluggish pituitary. Maybe it was polycystic ovaries or kidney trouble.

Or maybe it was something even worse, something fatal. It probably was. It made sense. Why screw around with diabetes when there were things like Huntington's disease to get people's attention? By the time I started grad school, my imaginary illnesses were routinely fatal, my symptoms 911-urgent. I began interrupting seminars to warn my classmates about an imminent stroke. At the time the body was the hot field in literary theory, so it didn't seem particularly off-topic. "I don't mean to derail this fascinating debate over Foucault, but I'm pretty sure an artery in my brain stem is about to blow," I'd announce, while my classmates stared. "I wanted to raise my hand now, before I lose motor control of my right side."

While I waited for the cerebral hemorrhage to fell me, some new symptom would arise to preoccupy me instead. It might be a headache (brain tumor), or leg cramps (Parkinson's). It could be a stuffy nose (sinus cancer) or dry mouth (lupus). Or maybe it would be something more literary. A cousin had recently developed pleurisy, a condition I thought had gone out of print with *Little Women*, and this had piqued my interest in the antiquated afflictions that cropped up in my reading. I hadn't known I could contract these, but maybe I could. Maybe I had Beth's scarlet fever, or Mimi's consumption. Maybe I had something tragic and poetic like porphyria or syphilis, a pretty-sounding terminal disease that would drive me slowly mad while inspiring poignant verse that would sell well after my death.

Or maybe it would be something less lyrical, something tacky and embarrassing. This seemed most likely. "I'm pretty sure it's toxic shock syndrome," I told my roommates when I got home from class, throwing down my backpack and producing sweaty palms, dry mouth, a pallor. "I know, it's so seventies, and so cheesy, making people think of tampons, tampons, tampons and all, but I'm really pretty sure that's what it is. Do you think you could drive me to the hospital after *Friends*?"

My roommates, psychology Ph.D. candidates, were inclined to blame my symptoms on stress and bad nutritional habits instead. "It's probably because you ate cinnamon Red Hots for dinner," they'd say gently. "Go eat a sandwich, lie down for a bit, and if you're seizing or comatose we'll see about a ride then."

When I was home alone with no one to talk me down, I called 911 instead. I'd been hoping for sympathy and was shocked to find operators so unlike the helpful ones I'd seen on *Oprah* being reunited with the accident victims whose lives they'd saved. Instead of modestly claiming they were just doing their jobs, these weary clock-punchers just barked at me. "I'm not going to discuss your history of suspected hypoglycemia with you," they snapped. "Do you want an ambulance or not?"

My father's technique for dealing with hypochondriacs was inspired by *The Story of San Michele*, the 1929 roman à clef about a Salpetrière doctor and his silly, privileged patients, all of them afflicted with nothing more serious than ennui. Rather than dismiss them, the doctor simply assigns a diagnosis and description of the symptoms they could expect. That, after all, is all they wanted in the first place, a new accessory their friends might cluck over sympathetically. The advantage, my father admitted, is that by doing this you can control the patient's symptoms. And if it turns out you're mistaken, that they're not hypochondriacal at all, and they surprise you by developing a symptom you didn't suggest, you have a good clue to what might actually be wrong.

What was wrong with me was too much time on my hands. But the method worked beautifully on me too. Once, when I got mysteriously and acutely sick, too weak to get out of bed, my father's diagnosis was swift and sure. "It's your thyroid," he told me, because it was less scary than the Lou Gehrig's disease I'd diagnosed on my own.

Within twenty-four hours I had developed all the symptoms of an overactive thyroid. My skin and hair were dry. My pulse was double its normal rate and my hands shook. I was short of breath. My reflexes were exaggerated. I had no appetite and I was losing weight. It was such a textbook case. "Aren't my eyes big?" I asked my friends. "It's what they call the 'thyroid stare.' They're just bugging on out. I look like Bette Davis, don't I?

Look, I'll do an impression. 'What a dump!' How was that? Pretty good, right?"

Another symptom of hyperthyroidism is annoying personality changes.

By the time the lab results came back showing normal thyroid levels I'd already recovered completely. Who knows what it really was. It was nothing.

It was usually nothing. But it always felt so real. It felt like I was dying, a slow or sudden death of whatever disease I'd settled on this time. And there were such realistic symptoms. By my second year of graduate school I'd managed to produce an irregular heartbeat, a careening rhythm that would shoot to 180 for no reason, then drop back down to 60. Maybe it was due to panic attacks, or maybe it was due to my bad habit of borrowing medication from one parent without informing the other, a practice that sometimes caused interesting drug interactions. I was, at the time, taking unprescribed Atenolol (a heart rate regulator) for tremors, and for some imaginary allergies, unprescribed Seldane, a drug that was taken off the market a short time later for producing a cardiac arrhythmia that killed people.

An erratic heartbeat is the sort of symptom that guarantees lots of tests. I had stress tests and echocardiograms. I wore a Holter monitor for a week. I'd discontinued my self-prescribed mix n' match pharmaceutical routine, but still, the episodes continued, once or twice a day. We had to get to the bottom of this. It wasn't right, a twenty-three-year-old girl having heart trouble. It could be a prolapsed valve, or maybe an adrenal tumor. Maybe it was my kidneys. On my doctor's orders I col-lected my urine in two-liter Diet Pepsi bottles I stored in the refrigerator, an exercise that revealed my roommates were in-deed very patient, but not why I was sick in the first place.

It was very exciting, all this fuss. My family, by now, knew better than to trust me when I complained about my health, but the electrical leads and specimen cups got them con-cerned. My grandparents clucked over me and checked in on me frequently. I loved them, but until then we hadn't had much in common. Now we were bound by our mutual heart conditions. "Come sit next to me and tell me about your an-gina," my grandfather would say, patting the couch next to him. "Let's talk about nitro tabs."

Even my father went along with it. What we needed, he thought, was a nice clear EKG during one of my episodes, something the Holter monitor had failed to capture very cleanly. Home for Thanksgiving I tried to will an attack. I fi-nally pulled it off in the middle of the turkey dinner, dashing off to the ER to get an EKG, heart pounding, returning home just in time for pie. It was a spectacular performance.

On some level, I knew that's all it was. Oh, I had an irregu-lar EKG all right. But I had also, by now, noticed that I could precipitate an attack, make my heart race wildly out of no-where. I also figured I could make it stop, but why, when ev-eryone was treating me so nicely, when the only downside was a refrigerator full of urine?

Yes, well, there was that. And on some level, I knew, I'd had enough. I suspected the Thanksgiving Day episode would be my last, and it was. I had other things to occupy me. By then I'd managed to rack up some incompletes so I returned my attention to my schoolwork, focusing on others' illnesses instead of my own. I wrote papers about Christina Rossetti's Graves' disease, Joyce's blindness, Virginia Woolf's clinical depression, Emily Dickinson's kidney trouble.

If I'd done a paper on my own sickness, on my hypochondria, I would have explored the ways that hypochondria is a disease of fictions, of symptoms that seem so real but lie. I might have contemplated all the work I was putting in maintaining the fiction that I was happy in graduate school when in fact I was miserable, cold, and lonely, utterly adrift in a discipline I didn't quite get. Because queer theory was big, I would have made hay of "brain fag," the somatic condition akin to Trinidadian "studiation madness" that West African students sometimes get when they are at school, homesick and overwhelmed. Then I would have unpacked the symbology and symptomology of homesickness itself. Maybe that, not heart trouble, is what I actually had.

In the conclusion I would have referenced *The Story of San Michele*, and called this strange disorder a lark, a froth to pass the time. It is a mystery, I would write, full of red herrings and false clues. It is a program that runs its course. It did, and by the time I left graduate school I felt fine. Well, fine for me.

Like many stories, this one would turn out to have sequels. Bouts would recur, procedures would be done, everything would be fine and then, once again, it would not.

But if hypochondria is fiction, fiction is malleable, and even in a textbook case, the author can choose her ending, happy or sad. I could take a page from *San Michele*'s Dr. Munthe and make up my own disease, assign my own symptoms. Munthe picked colitis; I would choose something with less GI distress, something flattering and curable, consumption perhaps.

I take to my boudoir like Camille. Propped up on my pillows in my satin bed jacket, I catch up on my reading. There's so much left to learn. Out come the medical encyclopedias and pharmaceutical handbooks, the surgical journals and insurance charts. It's time, once again, to study for my tests.

Fig. 8. Sycosis

9

The Best of
Everything

✿

My college fears of contagion were, it must be said, somewhat justified. Like many California institutions, UC Berkeley is clothing-optional. For years I'd struggled with the thought of who might have sat in my desk before me; now I had to wonder if they were wearing *pants*. It was not uncommon to see a freshman striding across campus wearing nothing but a backpack and Tevas, and several times a week you'd encounter the lesbian couple in matching fanny packs and ungroomed pubic hair. My own roommate belonged to a community of free spirits who wore only mud. Naked was somewhat normal. You learned quickly that you had every reason to bring your own Sani-Seat to lecture, and unless you knew exactly which kind they were referring to, when someone offered you nuts it was best just to say no.

The nakedness was just a symptom of Berkeley's general aesthetic, where the way-back machine is set perpetually to 1974. And in Berkeley's defense, that's not the worst decade to relive. The 1970s were the first decade of my life, and except for the streaking, it suited me just fine. I liked variety shows, and I look good in knee-high boots. Color TV had been invented already, and by the time I was ready to use them, both VCRs and Cuisinarts had been too.

The downside, of course, was growing up with all the children whose parents had hooked up in the Summer of Love. I sometimes wonder what our teachers thought that September in the mid-1970s when we all showed up at school, dropped off by parents in fringed vests and smoky sunglasses. My classmates had names like Rain, Meadow, Brandy, or Chardonnay, monikers that seemed to suggest the vaguely disturbing details of their conception. Their parents were organic farmers, belly dancers, and divorcées. They were New Age thinkers who allowed you to do anything, as long as you did it with them.

Mine did not. Although they met in San Francisco in the late sixties, my parents weren't hippies. Already in their late twenties, my parents were just a little too old for the flower child nonsense, but even if they'd been younger I think they still would have abstained. Far too pragmatic to take psychedelics, or even wear tie-dye, my parents were your responsible friends. They were the ones you called when sexual experimentation left you with a chair leg in your lower colon, or your five-day acid freakout found you naked in the back of a squad car. They didn't judge, but dropping out and tuning in just wasn't their thing.

By the time I came along, the only remnant of the era was a travel bag my mother kept in the back of her closet, whose logo urged "Fly LSD." It had been a gag gift. I suppose my

parents were squares, but that was just fine with me. Even as
a child, hippies wore me out. While I appreciated the liberty
to sniff markers at certain friends' houses, their free-thinking
parents embarrassed and exhausted me. It always seemed to
be about *them*. Every event was an excuse to tell me a story I
didn't want to hear. I didn't want to "rap" with them, didn't
want to share my feelings, didn't want to hear that our bodies
were changing and that was a beautiful thing. I didn't like their
unconditioned hair or their dirty feet, their Creedence Clear-
water or their self-righteous carob. My parents might be square,
but at least at my house you could eat a Ho Ho in peace.

What you couldn't do was spark a doob, a phrase I'm quite
sure I didn't learn at home. My family talked openly about anal
fissures, but we rarely discussed drugs, a topic that, unlike anal
fissures, would have embarrassed us all. I remember the subject coming up only twice. The first time was in fourth grade
when I asked my mother to explain the title of the book I was
reading, *Dinky Hocker Shoots Smack*. "Smack is chiva, the white
lady," my mother hastily replied, in an uncharacteristically nervous burst of over-information that would keep me from ever
raising the subject again. "You probably know it as horse."

The second time was when the networks ran PSAs urging
parents to discuss drug use with their kids. My father dis-
charged this obligation before the commercial ended. "If you
girls use drugs, I will kill you. Discussion over."

The fact that he gave this speech while drinking out of a
tumbler embossed with the logo of a prescription analgesic
sort of undercut the point. Street drugs might have been taboo

in our house, but the other kind was our bread and butter. I like to tell people I grew up on a pharm, because pharmaceutical companies supplied so much of our home's durable goods. They'd given us our coffee cups and stationery, our paperweights, clocks, calculators, and desk accessories. My parents had eloped, and this was the closest thing they had to a trousseau. At friends' houses I'd admire a punch bowl and be told it was a wedding gift from Aunt Pearl. Do the same at my house and my mother might smile fondly and sigh, "Bristol-Myers Squibb."

I came to think of Bayer, Pfizer, Eli Lilly, and Merck as generous uncles, distant but kind men who sent the sorts of lavish gifts you buy when you're rich and don't know the recipient very well. My friends got excited when the Avon lady dropped by, but I saved my enthusiasm for the drug company rep, the well-dressed pusher man with his briefcase full of freebies. The giveaways are more closely regulated now, but in the 1970s as I recall things were fairly loose. Pharmaceutical reps gave out great swag: cases of wine, bonbons, ashtrays, and lavish dinners. It seems worth noting that I even remember how often their gifts were bad for you, which made me suspect they wanted you not just to prescribe, but consume, the heart disease/liver failure/lung cancer/diabetes drugs they were planning to release later.

The most memorable goodies were part of a drug company promotion called "The Best of Everything." Once a month, we received a different sample of the world's best products: the world's best chocolate, preserves, brandy, soap. My mother normally bought off-brand products, so this was a big treat and allowed me to indulge my fantasies of being a pampered heiress. When the package would arrive, I would spend the next few days pretending I was a young deb, enjoying the high life that I'd somehow missed out on.

The enjoyment was somewhat tempered by the fact that we had been sent single-serving units of each item. This was fine for bachelor doctors, but in our house the treats had to be divided by four. I managed to feel pretty luxurious enjoying my allotted square of the world's best chocolate, but the illusion became harder to maintain when faced with my half teaspoon of the world's best jam. By the time I slipped into the shower with my sliver of the world's best soap the charade could no longer be maintained.

Still, as far as I was concerned, this was far better than the homespun presents we got from my father's patients. These gifts were sweet but clumsy, and while I know the thought counts, I think the price should count more. These were never bought, always handpicked or handmade. There was, for instance, the crocheted disc with elasticized edging we mistook for a very large, floppy hat. We all took turns trying it on, mugging and vamping, pretending to be P-Funk All-Stars. It wasn't until my mother received the reply to her thank-you note that we learned it was actually a toilet seat cover.

Many of my father's patients were farm folk, and we often received gifts of home-laid eggs, unpasteurized milk, and overripe zucchini. Once, for Christmas, a patient gave us some venison he'd shot himself. Because he did not say what it was or suggest that it might need to be refrigerated, it sat under the tree for two full weeks, the dog sniffing the merry wrapping with fierce intensity all the while. My father finally opened it on Christmas afternoon and found six pounds of warm, reeking deer meat topped by a thick hide of mold. It might have been the world's best rotten deer meat, but still, I preferred the goodies the drug companies sent over.

These included, of course, the drugs themselves. By age seven I already had a thing for them. For a hypochondriac child, drugs are better than candy. They're like sour apple schnapps: a fruit-flavored treat that makes you feel grown up. Perhaps because we often got them free, my sister and I took far more prescription meds than most healthy children do. We started the day with an orangey chewable fluoride tablet, washed down with Tang we pretended was a mimosa. "I sure need my important medicine this morning after that big party we went to last night," we might say. "Don't talk to me until it kicks in because I've got a hangover like you wouldn't believe." Down the hatch and the day would begin, our Looney Toons juice glasses raised in a toast to the best of everything.

Time was marked by the administration of drugs. Midday meant the application of any number of steroidal ointments for my various skin conditions. Bedtime was toasted with a grape-flavored narcotizing antihistamine nightcap. Because it was delicious, we developed a taste for it and took more than we actually needed, which was none. Because it made bedtime go that much more smoothly, our parents didn't stop us, and because it was medicine, no one worried about it. Honestly, it's a wonder I wasn't shooting the white lady right into my neck vein by junior high.

Or maybe it wasn't; as much as I enjoyed the prescription drugs, the other kind held no appeal for me. It was partly that I suspected they had something to do with the reason certain friends' parents were so annoying, and partly because the antidrug message had sunk in so deeply. When I was thirteen I'd been blown right out of my seat by antidrug crusader/motivational powerhouse David Toma. The town school board had flown him in and for weeks leading up to the event it had been all anyone could talk about.

"Toma's coming," our teachers began threatening, whenever there was back talk. "Toma will set you straight." It almost seemed worth developing a drug problem just to have the privilege. The man was famous. As the real-life model for *Baretta* he was, hands down, the biggest celebrity ever to pay us a visit. This was such a big deal that every student from age twelve to eighteen was crammed into a gym to hear what the man had to say.

We'd never seen anyone like this, a real New Jersey Eye-talian, here to tell us stories from the front lines of the drug war. There was the young mother, high on acid, who'd confused her baby for a roast and baked it, and the honor student who'd lost it all over angel dust. All around me my cooler classmates snickered while I listened, rapt. Were they deaf? Were they blind? This stuff was *gold.*

At the dinner table that night I recounted how great he'd been. "The man's a genius, and his message was right-on." My sister, who'd been among the snickerers earlier, rolled her eyes at me now. "I feel sorry for you," I told her. "I listened. I *learned*. And now I know for a fact that I will never try drugs because *drugs kill*." With that, I drank my quarter-cup of prescription cough syrup, stormed off to bed, and slept like a zombie, my eyes shielded by a satin pillow advertising a newly released anti-insomnia medication.

If this was hypocrisy it did not occur to me; we were blinded by the swag. But all parties have to end, and within a few years this one was wrapping up. "That damn Ted Kennedy," my mother spat every time she had to pay for her own stemware. In the 1990s he would spearhead legislation to end drug company payola, but the goods had started to dry up even before then. By the mid-1980s all we got were things like notepads, key chains, and refrigerator magnets, and of course, the drugs themselves, all useful but except for the latter, without any resale value. Every pen and notepad in our home bore the name of a medication. I snickered when my parents warned "BE HOME BEFORE MIDNIGHT" on a note advertising birth control, and cringed when they sent my teachers letters on stationery promoting antidiarrheals. Once my biology teacher noticed the logo on one such note and shared memories of his own youth as a doctor's son, when they would burn the drug samples in the fireplace and watch the pretty colors.

By my generation, we'd learned to watch the pretty colors by taking the drugs instead, especially at Berkeley, where, true to its reputation, I was offered drugs within two hours of moving into my dorm. By 1988, drug use was no longer a graduation requirement, but still, college is college. It was rumored that at one student housing complex "LSD" was painted in giant letters on the carport, to remind would-be jumpers that they were tripping, and not actually able to fly. You'd occasionally come across a disoriented sky-high grad student moaning in an ivy bed, or a group of chemistry majors putting their education to use building beaker bongs. These things happened. The PC climate on campus created an environment where placing something like nonunion grapes in your mouth was an unthinkable sin, while stuffing in a sheet of acid was a perfectly reasonable thing to do. But really, by 1988, it was no wilder than any other campus, and probably tamer than many.

Clearly, though, it wasn't BYU. I'd never done drugs before, but it was a smooth enough transition. By then the Toma fervor had worn off, and drugs had never scared me that much, anyway. Because of my close, lifelong relationship with drug companies, I have complete and perfect faith in pharmochemicals. I will swallow anything in a gelcap. This is a trait I've noticed is very common among doctors' children, and the reason some of us find ourselves suddenly popular in college.

I did not. My drug career was enthusiastic but clumsy, distinguished mostly by my complete failure to look cool or have any fun at all. I am the person barfing in your car; the girl who announces she's *so high* until she finds out the brownies are, in fact, just brownies; the moron who will spend forty dollars on talcum powder. The impressive stash of drugs I received for graduation was in my body for less than an hour before I projectile-vomited it onto my friends, art majors, who recorded the scene as a comic panel they sent out later that year as a Christmas card.

Because my drug experimentation was so unsuccessful, it was, happily, brief, and by the time I left for graduate school I'd learned to medicate my feelings with a cocktail and the occasional cadged Percocet like any normal adult. This meant I was probably sober when I made one of the worst decisions of my adult life. I was in my early twenties and had just spent a year in the most depressing example of graduate student housing on the Eastern seaboard. My mother had moved me into several dumps by this point—she'd once dropped me off at a new house where we found a "Neighborhood Stabbing Alert!" flyer waiting like a welcome mat on the front stoop— but this was the first time she actually hesitated to leave me. The apartment was dangerous only in an aesthetic sense, all industrial carpet and concrete walls, but it still seemed potentially fatal, an invitation to suicidal despair. "This is the bleakest apartment I've ever seen in my life," she'd sighed, as she backed out toward the rental car. "It looks like an airport terminal in Beirut." Living there did, in fact, feel like an extended layover, a miserable interval to endure until summer came and I could go back to California, broken up by trips to Cinnabon and a lot of CNN.

June came and what I needed, clearly, was altered states. I had to get back to the Bay Area. A friend of a friend knew of a

San Francisco sublet. It was with some students, she said, and it wasn't in the *best* neighborhood, but there was always something going on and it was sure to be fun. Was I interested? I was. The deal was sealed over the phone and two weeks later, I moved into what I quickly realized was something approaching a drug den.

I probably should have expected this. At the time, if you sublet a furnished room in the Bay Area it was more than likely the furnishings would include at least one six-way bong. San Francisco has always been, in the local parlance, 420-friendly, and in the mid-1990s it was especially so, with the rave scene still going and heroin chic on the way in. It was just the place, and the time, and you considered yourself lucky if your sublet's bathtub had not been commandeered for hydroponic pot-growing.

Now, in fairness to all concerned, I never actually saw my new roommates take any drugs, and I am not trained like Toma to identify who's "using." Nor, however, did I see people sleep. Here's what I did see plenty of: microscopic pupils, unexplained sores, jaws clenched so tight they could have stamped lead. In that apartment that summer, people came and went, and I didn't get to know any of them very well, but some of them seemed to share the same hobbies: grinding their teeth, examining their pores, creating art from dental floss, and staying up all night to execute home improvement projects. Their favorite activity was moving furniture, and every other morning I'd wake up to find the couch in a different place.

Though I'm not a drug user, like most addicts, I do live in

denial, and I tried to convince myself it would be okay. This was not the summer I'd planned, but maybe it wouldn't be so bad. I wasn't home that much. During the days I temped, and at night, well, at least there might be people to hang out with. Within a week of moving in I'd realized that all my college friends had scattered, gone off to kayak in Costa Rica or teach tennis to underprivileged Basques. My new roommates weren't home much, often disappearing for days, but when they were there you could be sure they were doing something entertaining. Eleven p.m.? Let's make an aluminum-foil carpet for the living room! Two a.m.? Time to move the couches!

You never knew where the night might lead. Once, after joining them for a beer, I woke up and found myself in a dental chair, being propositioned by a dwarf. Apparently I'd just innocently dozed off, tired from my early-morning temp job, but this sort of thing happened when you hung out at our crash pad. Even Sunday brunch was interesting. I'd expected nothing more than Bloody Marys, so I was a bit surprised to find myself sharing a table with the sort of fellow whom cop shows call "the supplier," leading what appeared to be a staff meeting. The supplier was a heavyset gangbanger with, apparently, shared custody. His toddlers ran around the pub while their daddy explained the difference between your good-quality shit and your cold medicine and explained how things would be going down that week.

I'm not sure when it was, exactly, that things started to go downhill, but I think it was around the time of the barbecue. There had been some vodka-soaked watermelon, and the usual migration of the couches. Some people dropped by with a case of beer. Out came the guitars for a jam session, and by late afternoon the furniture had been moved into the backyard and set on fire.

I called my mother. "They're burning a chifforobe."

"A chifforobe? What's wrong with these people? A footstool, I could see, but a chifforobe is nuts. Maybe you should spend the rest of the summer at home."

I did not tell her about the shotgun I'd seen lying on a bed the night before.

I did not tell her, a week later, when strangers took up residence in the living room. They were, a subletter said with a dismissing wave, friends of friends who needed a place to crash. These were people who, if I were to conjecture, had escalated their drug use to a point where they could no longer pay rent, and were now taking up residence on our remaining couches, turning our living room into a bus station with plaid upholstery. By the looks of them, they could soon pass for prostitutes and hoboes, but for now they were my houseguests.

The most notable guest was a stocky, unwashed Slav named Dimebag. Dimebag was missing several teeth and sported a fine collection of self-administered tattoos. He did not appear to have a regular job, but his pager's constant activity suggested that drugs might be more of a profession than a hobby.

I'd never lived with a drug dealer before. I'd expected a little more creepy glamour, frankly. College friends told stories about going to their pot dealer's house and it always seemed to involve strange snacks and exotic pets; they'd get stuck there for a couple hours, eating cocktail onions, waiting for the dealer to tube-feed a snake. All Dimebag did was lie on the couch in dirty camo pants, watching talk shows and eating burritos. The straitlaced drug reps of my youth had been more exciting. They'd certainly been more generous. Dimebag offered no notepads or key chains, no swag of any kind, unless you counted the earwax-stained Q-tips and fingernail clippings someone habitually left on the coffee table. The best of everything, I thought, was using a magazine subscription card to brush them onto the carpet.

The denial was beginning to wear off. This was an awful, awful summer. Every morning I left the house at six-thirty in jumpers and collared shirts to spend the day in a horrible office. Every night I came home and locked myself in my room with a library book and a loaf of bread, my drugs of choice, my buffer against the craziness without.

A year earlier MTV had been in town to film *The Real World*. At houses like mine the show was more compelling: see what happens when people stop being polite, and start burning the furniture, hiding the mail, picking sores on their legs, and storing valuables in their assholes.

Things had turned. A pall of paranoia hung over the house like the bay fog that rolled in every afternoon. Some roommates installed padlocks on their bedroom doors, sealing them shut like gym lockers every time they left the house. When they were home, they might keep close to the front window to monitor suspicious activity outside.

There was, in their defense, plenty of suspicious activity

to monitor. We lived near the city's largest encampment of unmedicated psychotics, and it was not unusual to see a gentleman wearing a shopping bag as a hat or taking a dump in a dryer.

Still, I didn't think any of the suspicious characters were undercover narcs, or DEA agents, or disgruntled drug dealers, and chalked the fears up to paranoia. And when I got a call at my temp job, telling me not to come home, I wasn't quite sure what to do. One resident had convinced everyone it had gotten much too risky to sleep there, apparently, and they'd all decided to clear out for the night.

When you live someplace like that, every situation boils down to one simple question: is this true, or is it your crazy paranoid fantasy? There is usually evidence for both sides, and making the call becomes an art. There probably isn't a transmitter in the kitchen faucet, but the trash can ant invasion might be real. It was true that strange things happened all the time. One night the bathroom doorknob disappeared. A week later, an extraordinary backup in the toilet formed; a plumber was called, and it was discovered the knob had been *flushed*.

As I had learned to do over the past several weeks, I weighed potential danger against imaginary threat and decided it was probably fine. I went home and spent the night in the apartment by myself. It was the best sleep I'd gotten in six weeks.

I do not believe in the concept of a contact high, but living in this flophouse, the drugs started to seep in. I never touched a needle—the strongest thing I ingested all summer was half an Ativan—but the drugs got under my skin all the same. Of course they did. I was a hypochondriac, a medical mockingbird who can't help but mimic others' side effects and symptoms. I became paranoid and restless, picked at my skin. When I looked in a mirror I didn't recognize myself. This was the cliché, the trope of every antidrug after-school special. In my case it was just because I was wearing the crisp separates my temp jobs demanded, but still. This wasn't me.

That, I suppose, is why we take drugs, street or legal. They make you feel different. If you're sick, they make you feel well. If you're uncomfortable in your skin, they soothe the pricking. They make you feel like someone else. They make you the deb enjoying the best of everything, the society doyenne washing her important pill down with a mimosa, the lame girl barfing in your car.

But they only change who you are while you're on them. In a sense, all drugs are topical, skin deep, treating the symptom but not the self. Take me out of my work separates, out of my drug den, and I was the same person I was when I was seven: a straight arrow who didn't much care for hippies or drugs, the illegal kind, anyway. I wouldn't have wanted to admit it, but I was a square, just like my parents.

Later that summer my sister and I would go home to visit our parents and we'd be subjected to an intense interrogation over the plant with five-pointed leaves that had mysteriously sprung up in their backyard. The four of us squatted in the flower bed, Vicky and I agreeing with our parents that it sure looked like pot but insisting we had no idea how it got there. It is testament to our collective innocence that we didn't even know what pot looked like. "Japanese maple," the gardener finally informed us, shaking his head. We laughed, ha-ha, drugs are funny, and then we went back inside to get into the really good prescription antihistamines.

But even prescription drugs will only help so much. I wasn't happy in my sublet-cum-crash pad, and it was, it seemed, time to alter my states again. Every day I walked by the landmarks of the Summer of Love, and like my parents had twenty-five years earlier, I knew it wasn't my scene either. There was the McDonald's where my mother had to collect a hallucinating former high school classmate clad in nothing but a fur coat; there was the grocery store where they bought frozen peas to ice the drug-related bruises and cuts. It's not fun being the sober one at the drug party. By now, it was August, and I got ready to go.

Toward the end of the summer Jerry Garcia died. One of my friends was in town, and that night we meandered down Haight Street to see the impromptu memorial. It was like the Vatican after the pope's death, the believers massed to mourn their fallen idol. Everywhere you looked there were clusters of sobbing hippies, clutching ragged bouquets illegally gathered from nearby Golden Gate Park. Makeshift altars had sprung up on every corner and twinkling votives lined the sidewalks. The cause of death, of course, had been drug abuse, which made it either ironic or fitting when doobs were sparked in his honor, as they were, every few feet, by men in tie-dyed broom skirts and girls in Holly Hobbie frocks.

"What are all the Deadheads going to do now?" my friend

wondered. We kicked around ideas: maybe we should start a cult for them, or a nonprofit to mainstream them back into normal society. Maybe we'd open up the first all-Deadhead temp agency. We'd bathe and shave them, put shoes on their wide, dirty, archless feet, teach them to type, and send them out into the workforce at 40 percent commission. On holidays, we'd send them gifts, coffee cups, and pens embossed with the agency logo.

These are the thoughts you have when the air is 25 percent oxygen, 75 percent party fumes: pipe dreams. Instead I just went back to Boston. The Deadheads followed Phish, and life went on. I lost touch with my quasi-roommates, which is to say I fled and didn't leave a forwarding address.

But we still had some mutual friends of friends of friends, and a few years later I'd heard how a few of them were doing. They were well, sober, studying, employed. I, of course, was still hooked on my drugs of choice—anxiety, medical diction-aries, and Neosporin—but it would take more than a stint in rehab to get me off those.

Sometimes I think about my old housemates, and how they were then, how I was too. "If you remember it, you weren't there," the saying goes. I remember it, so I guess I wasn't, and in any case, I'd rather forget. It's an unpleasant flashback. In-stead, I turn back further, to 1982. It's March. The highest-quality pralines in the world have just arrived. And I know that everything, just everything, will work out for the best.

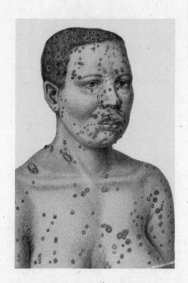

Fig. 9. Pustular Syphilis

Shake It Up

✱

My relatives and I do not share a strong resemblance, but at family parties you can tell who the Traigs are by the vibrating drinks, the shaking of our hands making blenders unnecessary. We have what doctors call an "essential tremor." "Essential" means it's not attributable to any disease; it's not Parkinson's or MS, and it doesn't have a real cause or effect. It's annoying, but more or less benign, and it doesn't really bother any of us. Perhaps because we live in California, where it's not unusual for things to start shaking for no reason, we're fairly indifferent to it. Mine does not impact my life in any significant way except that strangers will sometimes remark that it looks like Mama needs her Xanax.

Like most of my problems, this one starts in my head. Unlike my hypochondria, however, it's an actual medical condition. Essential tremor begins in the brain, caused by a malfunction in the central oscillator and inferior olivary nucleus, which is not, apparently, as tasty as it sounds but has something to do with the brain stem. This seems scary but isn't, and the condition is neither dangerous nor rare. It's the most common neurological movement disorder, treatable with drugs and made worse by stress. For some reason alcohol usually helps, as do, in my experience, cupcakes.

Essential tremor is also known as "familial tremor," and it runs very strongly among relations. In my family exactly half of us have it, down to the pets. The cat, no; the dog, yes. His tremor was not actually essential but epileptic, but either way we never tired of making "shake, boy" jokes.

Even babies can have the disorder. It usually shows up later in life, but can appear at any time. Mine first surfaced when I was in graduate school. There was a little stress, and a lot of loneliness, and I kept getting sick, or at least thinking I was. A few months into it I went to a family wedding, with my parents and sister and aunts and uncles and cousins, and I was so happy to see everyone I was shaking with excitement. And then I was shaking with subdued happiness, and then I was shaking with mild boredom, and then, six hours later, I was still shaking for no reason at all.

This may have had something to do with the extraordinary amount of intoxicants I consumed. Though we've all become the boring clean-living types we once considered losers, there was a time my cousins and I viewed family gatherings as a prescription-meds swap meet. As I recall, one of my cousins had recently met a nurse, so this gathering was more interesting than usual, involving the sorts of drugs that are normally reserved for hospice patients. Because I was trying to shake an intractable flu, I'd added a grab bag of antibiotics and antihistamines to the mix, washing it all down with an open bar.

My cousins kept up with me and by two a.m. we were conducting drunken human wheelbarrow races, dragging each other by the ankles through the Berber-carpeted hallways of the staid Virginia golf resort. By three a.m. I should have been passed out by my door, having lost the key, but instead, I was awake and shaking like a Chihuahua.

Well, *this* was new. Alcohol normally masks a tremor, but combined with a lot of other things and no sleep it can, apparently, bring it into stark relief, and suddenly, there I was, unable to hold my Mickey's Widemouth without sloshing it all over my pretty green dress.

The next morning I was more concerned about the rug burns on my legs where my taffeta had ridden up than I was about the tremors that had seized me for hours, which would be a regular part of my life from that time on. I was so used to seeing my relatives shake that it seemed only natural I'd inherit it at some point, a physical family heirloom like crow's feet or copious nose hair. Despite my hypochondria, this didn't scare me at all. Hypochondria was terrifying because you didn't know *what* was coming. It could be cancer or lupus or Lou Gehrig's disease. The shakes, however, were expected, and they were just shakes.

So what troubled me was not the "tremor" but the "essential." In academia, "essentialism" was, at that time, a dirty word, about the worst thing you could say about another scholar. You could call someone an "ignorant motherfucker" and they'd just raise an eyebrow and say something pithy about Oedipus, but "essentialist" was a declaration of war, a true epithet. It meant that things were what they were: me Tarzan, you Jane. Calling someone "essentialist" was like calling them a caveman. It insinuated that you knew they were lying about not owning a TV, and that you suspected they used it to watch *Wheel of Fortune*. Essentialism was a square and backward philosophy, the academic equivalent of an *L* to the forehead.

The opposite of essentialism was deconstructionism, an altar we were to worship by smashing its very foundations. We were shaking things *up*. Deconstructionism said that nothing was fixed, not even gender or race; we were all just performing the roles the Man had cast us in. Oh, and there was no Man. There was no male, no female, just an assortment of tropes indicating one or the other, a costume and accessories to be donned or doffed at will. A penis was no more meaningful than a purse.

Deconstructionism had prevailed for twenty years or so at this point, and by the 1990s it had started to feel like a passé rebellion, like bobby-soxing or bra-burning. It was on its way out, but we didn't know that yet. We clung to it like a life raft even as we noticed that the female professors were the only ones who had breast pumps in their offices, and if race didn't matter, why were we embarrassed that we were all white?

For one class we actually had to come in drag. And so we did, the men gangly in their girlfriends' jersey dresses and lipstick, the women not fooling anyone in fedoras and ties. To further invert our usual roles we had decided it would be funny if we wore the professor's clothes. This turned out not to be subversive or funny so much as profoundly creepy. The whole thing was creepy. Deconstructionism had encouraged us to rethink our definition of attractiveness but photos from that class told the essential truth: we were not cute.

Bodies betray. I knew this better than anyone, my hands a trembly blur as I repositioned the professor's hat on my head. No wonder we wanted to believe in deconstructionism, dreaming of a life of pure theory, a world in which our brains floated in jars.

Drag. Good gracious. This was not what I'd been expecting. I had gone to graduate school hoping I would read and do book reports for a few years, then be handed a tenure-track position. It turned out to be very little literature and all literary theory. You only read novels, if you read them at all, to use them as a jumping-off point to prove the theory that the reader was a figment of the metatext, or a marginalized figment of the dis-placed author, or something else I didn't quite understand. Generally this involved lots of parentheses, colons, and corny double entendres. You tended to write papers with titles like "That's What *(S)he* Said: Feminist (In)tercourse in the Patri-archal Tongue," and you used a lot of words like "normative," "hegemony," and "topoi."

I also used the words "cocksucker," "asshole," and "ball sweat." Deconstructionism said that words had no fixed mean-ing or value, and I took this as license to swear freely. Shy and prudish, by age twenty-two I'd used four-letter words only a handful of times, but now, suddenly, I was an OED of vulgar talk. This didn't go over particularly well with people outside the English department, to whom these words had firmly fixed meanings that weren't at all positive. My boss at the bookstore where I worked over breaks had to take me aside for a talking-to. "Now, I'm all for freedom of speech, and I don't mind a well-placed swear. But can you refrain from shouting 'bitch tits' in front of the customers?"

Even my salty-tongued mother blanched. "Did you have to tell my bridge group the cheesecake was 'fucking awesome'?" she demanded. "Isn't 'delicious' descriptive enough?"

Secretly, the word *I* found distasteful was "theory." Besides the stuff about profanity—which I suspected I'd misinterpreted—the awful truth was that I didn't understand any of it. It was just so opaque and confusing, with sentences that went on for miles and led nowhere I could follow. I'd learned to read from magazines like *Glamour* and *Seventeen*. Unless an article has workout tips and a checklist of dos & don'ts, it's just not going to sink in.

Also, on some level, it all struck me as a load of crap. Meme, really? This was an actual thing? Diaeresis? Wasn't that what you got from eating too much fruit? Subtext sure, and metatext okay, but supertext is just something someone made up. And what did it matter, all this mental masturbation about the reader's perception of the author and the author's perception of the moment the reader recognizes the duality of his authority and subjectivity within the larger conception of society with its unstable markers, blah, blah, blah, just shoot me in the head. It was insufferable. It made no sense. I couldn't distinguish sign, signifier, and signified. I couldn't tell text from *texte,* subject from object from abject. I never could wrap my mind around the concept of the Lacanian "j/e," the split self, and attempts to do so left me with nothing more than a splitting headache.

In class I generally kept my mouth shut. I didn't understand what was going on, and even when I did, which was never, I could not pronounce the names: Lukács, Irigiray, Cixous, Bakhtin, Gayatri Chakravorty Spivak. It took me a full semester to realize "Fichte" and "Veekda" were actually the same person. Hadn't a Bob Thompson ever had a good idea? Weren't there any smart Amys? It made me doubt the very foundation of deconstructionism, that names were arbitrary; that a rose by any other name could still get tenure at Johns Hopkins. Clearly, there would never be a Professor Kylie or a Chad, Ph.D.

And yet somehow Jenny was expected to complete her term papers. Worse, she was expected to deliver them at conferences. I delivered exactly one, titled, all too accurately, "Signifying Nothing." The only thing I remember is shaking a lot while I read it.

Twenty pages is a long time to go on about something you don't get at all. My papers tended to follow an established formula that involved two-inch margins and heavy quoting.° Be-

°Also, a shocking number of footnotes. These I loved because they made you look scholarly and they also took up lots of room. Sure, the print was smaller, but the standards were more lax; as long as it was prefaced by a tiny asterisk, you could pad with whatever you wanted—rap lyrics or cereal nutrition facts or celebrity gossip—and call it "meta." My footnotes, fittingly, tended to be pedestrian, no-duh observations that seemed somehow smarter in tiny type. My favorite thing to comment on was anatomy. Since

cause it took up half a page, I always opened with a definition: "The dictionary defines reading as: 1. the act of comprehending a text; 2. the act of comprehending a text aloud; 3. the act of comprehending a text aloud, in front of an audience. 4.—" It is a fact that my professor once commented in the margins, "Well, duh."

Well, duh. Fucking literary theory. I had a few theories. One was that I was wasting a lot of time and not a little money. This turned out to be right. That I had no business being an academic became quite clear when it came time to teach. Because we were cheap labor, all graduate students were assigned a few sections of Freshman Composition. It was a fine arrangement for my tweedy thirtysomething classmates, but for me it was just

---

body theory was so popular at the time, you could totally get away with this. Text-as-body was pretty huge. After all, a book has all these anatomical parts: a spine, an appendix, headers, and, of course, footers; it's bound in hide, and in a couple infamous cases, in actual human skin. It's a rich vein (anatomical reference again) and when you didn't have anything else to say you could go on and on about the physicality of the text itself, then go even more meta and comment on the very thing you were doing, the practice of, essentially (ha!) judging the book by the cover, a masturbatory (anatomical reference again) tangent that could fill up a good page and a half. And if your theory was half-assed (anatomical reference again), if you didn't have a leg to stand on (this is too easy, I can't help myself) you could comment on that too.

My ultimate dream was to deliver a paper in which all the footnotes were *actually about feet.* I was dying to tell this story, all true, about the time my sister came to Massachusetts to visit. She was staying with my cousin in the suburbs and they decided to hitchhike into Boston to save the eighty-five-cent T fare. One blonde, one redhead, both pretty and young, they were picked up within seconds by a big rig. The truck driver drove them to their requested drop-off point without protest, then locked the doors and delivered a speech they later suspected he gave on a near-daily basis.

"Now, I did you girls a pretty big favor, going out of my way to drive you to your stop in the snow and whatnot. I ain't going to ask for any money, but I think you-all owe me and now you're going to have to do me a favor too."

dangerous. This was the early 1990s, I was in my early twenties, and I had no sense of propriety. Because graduate school was blowing my mind like bad acid, like a twenty-four-hour rave, I came to teach dressed like Lady Miss Kier, all decked out in everything short of a Dr. Seuss hat. "A person needs so much cultural capital to understand what you're wearing," my adviser said one time, watching me waddle off to class in funkadelic boots and a lacy pink dress whose babyish cut and old food stains suggested I'd borrowed it from a toddler. I spent far more time planning my outfits than my lessons, a fact that would be clearly reflected when my course evaluations came back at the end of the semester. "I didn't really learn anything, but I liked her shoes," one said.°°

Vicky and Maureen steeled themselves and exchanged horrified glances.
"I want you to give me your socks."
At this point Vicky and Maureen did the only thing they could do and burst out laughing.
"I mean it, girls. Hand over them socks."
When it became clear they weren't getting out of the truck any other way, Maureen complied, removing her hiking boots and peeling off her sweat socks. Vicky just leaned back in the seat. "Sorry, can't help you there," she said, and gestured to her skirt. "I'm not wearing socks. I'm wearing tights." The trucker's eyes got wide and he sucked in his breath. "No, that's even better," he said, his voice tight.
"You're kidding. You want my *tights?*"
"Give me the tights."
"I'm not giving you my tights."
"I think you are."
"No."
"Give me the damn tights."
Two minutes later, Vicky and Maureen jumped out of the truck's cab and into the snow, barelegged in twenty-degree weather, and ran to the nearest department store, where they ended up spending fourteen dollars on new socks and tights. They took the T home.

°°Again with the feet. I'm just saying.

My only consolation was that a few other graduate students seemed to be doing the same thing. I read their remarkable outfits as cries of protest, a system of representation that, unlike theory, I understood. There was the philosophy grad student who wore Barbie costumes, and the Tyrolean linguist sporting short-short suede lederhosen in the middle of the Boston winter. I'd see them wandering across the quad, their thighs goosepimpling in the cold, and think, *mon semblable, mon frère*, then wonder if that phrase really meant what I thought it meant.

But surely even these oddly dressed colleagues were better teachers than I was; surely they had their act together in ways I could not hope for. I was utterly, profoundly incompetent. At the time, this university was the most expensive school in the country, and I wanted to personally refund each of my students' tuition checks for getting stuck with me. I considered sending notes of apology to the parents, knowing that their children would never learn enough composition to compose the letters themselves.

Within the first few weeks, I realized I was in over my head and met with the faculty supervisor, asking for help. His response was the simplest sentence I would ever hear an academic use, a theory that even I could grasp. "Two choices," he announced. "Sink or swim."

Instead, I came up with a third option: shake. The tremors that had seized me at my cousin's wedding were now showing up every Tuesday at 2:05, as I dragged myself to my three-hour Freshman Comp seminar. I'm not sure what set me off. I suppose it was the fact that I didn't know what I was doing, coupled with nerves. I'd never been particularly plagued by stage fright, but the thought of capturing the approval of twenty eighteen-year-olds just did me in. At the time I was watching a lot of *90210,* and while my students had little in common with the tanned, self-assured students of West Beverly High, they still intimidated me terribly. Surely they were rolling their eyes at me every time I turned to write something on the board, their jaded sighs riffling through their heavily hair-sprayed bangs. The pressure brought my tremor to a full rolling boil. If Brenda and Kelly saw me shake, I knew, it was over.

At first I tried to hide it. It seemed easy enough; all I would have to do was not use my hands. After a couple weeks of passing out papers with my elbows and grabbing my water bottle with my teeth, it became clear I was going to have to medicate myself in some way. Alcohol was out; it controlled the tremor beautifully but unloosed my tongue, and made me likely to say things like, "This one time, in college, I did something *I never thought I'd do.*" Herbs didn't work, and visualization was a waste of time.

When prescription medications failed, I ran out of options. So if I was going to shake, I decided, I might as well shake things up. Who would notice some shaking hands when there was porn on the overhead? Who would care about a little tremor when there was free candy?

I would distract my students with my unorthodox teaching style. I would stick it to the Man with my radical pedagogy. Tests? Term papers? Not for us! We were doing things differently in Freshman Comp Section 213. We were in the class-room called life, and that meant turning things upside down. It meant asking questions. Like, why not teach class wearing an apron and hot pants? Why sit inside a lecture hall when we could go down to the basement and try to knock free sodas out of the vending machines? Why not take a few weeks off?

Why read when we could watch TV? Why discuss Melville when we could spend forty-five minutes rehashing Billy and Amanda's recent relationship problems? Melville was just as important as *Melrose Place*, after all. Deconstructionism did away with artificial constructs of class and quality. There was no high culture or low; you could read meaning into anything, ads or cereal box copy, sitcoms or nighttime soaps. It was all a form of literature, it was all art. Instead of grammar, we would discuss Kelsey Grammer. Instead of spelling, Aaron Spelling, and extra credit would be given to students who came to class prepared to discuss that week's plot points on his shows.

Because I didn't understand theory but did get cable, I pro-grammed class like *TV Guide*, breaking it into entertaining half-hour segments. When we were done with the Melrose Minute we moved on to Conjunction Hokey Pokey. Next was Tattoo Show & Tell, followed by a forty-minute snack break. Because reading aloud could kill a lot of minutes I was also very fond of Storytime. Sometimes we read children's books, but more often the fare was decidedly adult. I was partial to politically charged women writers of the 1970s and frequently recited from works like Helen Gurley Brown's *Having It All* and

Marabel Morgan's *The Total Woman*, especially the parts that involved oral sex or greeting your man in plastic wrap.

Once a semester, during midterms, the academic equivalent of sweeps, we interrupted our regularly scheduled programming for the crowd favorite, Ask Me Anything. This was prefaced by my earnest declaration that the classroom was a safe space where students could ask whatever they wanted; there were no dumb questions. They quickly proved me wrong. I'd been expecting queries about my position on gender-neutral language, or using split infinitives as a political strategy. Questions I was actually asked included "What's your cup size?" and "So when a lady—um, farts from her vagina during sex? Is that actual gas or just air?"

Well, I only had myself to blame. I had deconstructed the classroom. I was shaking things *up*. I wish I could say that it was a theoretical stance, my bad teaching habits, my questionable pedagogy, but the truth is I didn't know what I was doing. I was only four years older than my students, trembling at the blackboard in a red vinyl mini-overall dress and tiny backpack, still trying to be the cool babysitter, the popular senior, desperately hoping they'd think my shakes were from DTs and not nerves. There I was, trying to hold the chalk between my elbows, hoping to impress them with my swears. "Fucking Melville, you guys. Fucking *Melville*." I just wanted them to like me.

Many of them did. Because I didn't take attendance or penalize late papers, and was incapable of giving grades lower than a B−, I became very popular among a certain class of students. By a less open-minded instructor they would have been called "cheaters," but I rejected the Man's tired labels. Wasn't cheating a culturally specific concept? Many of my students came from other countries and it didn't seem fair to impose our Western definitions of "copying" and "plagiarism" on them. Even when their offenses were blatant, I blamed societal constructs. Surely this student had simply been shaped by the customs of his country; it wasn't fair of me to judge. And apparently, in Florida, where this particular student came from, it was perfectly acceptable to lift your entire term paper right out of the issue of *Time* magazine *that was still on the stands.*

By midterms my class would devolve into *Lord of the Flies.* Students sometimes came to class drunk, waving adulterated cans of Coke whose fumes made my eyes water. They stopped turning in assignments, showed up in pajamas, or didn't show up at all. Class discussion mutated from an open exchange of ideas to a forum for venting their complaints about each other.

"Rachel has heavy calves."

"Okay, but we're discussing *Models Inc.* right now."

"I'm just saying. Also, Josh slept with my roommate? And he didn't call her back."

Absent an authority figure, my students turned on each other, then on me. By the last few weeks I'd be wondering if it would set off the sprinklers when the last bit of order broke down and they roasted a boar.

Somehow this went on for several years. Every once in a while I'd be called before a disciplinary board, asked to explain why I'd canceled three weeks of classes or led my students on a field trip to the snack bar, but for the most part, I had free rein. Here, I suppose, was proof of the limits of deconstructionism, of the reluctance to question the sign: everyone called me a teacher, so they thought I was.

But some students were smarter than that, and eventually one called me out. I'd gone to some ridiculous dance club in Cambridge on Alternative Sexuality Night. It was an unofficial field trip with my fellow graduate cross-dressers, deconstructionist fieldwork. The girl in the clear plastic breastplate collecting the cover fee was *living* literary theory. The pockmarked drag queen slipping off his bar stool was deconstructionism in heels.

We'd been there an hour or so when there, amid the bisexual high school students with fake IDs, semiprofessional dominatrices, and awkward MIT students, I spotted one of my students. He was by himself, leaning quietly against a column, watching me pogo while my colleagues pretended not to know me. The alcohol kept my tremor under control, but making a fool of myself on the dance floor, with my hair in Pam Dawber bunches and my legs in kneesocks, I did not appear to be particularly stable. I looked exactly like my essential self: a confused fuck-up trying way too hard.

It wasn't a blackmailable offense, but there, drinking fuzzy navels, I'd shown my soft belly. In class I was Teacher, but in this club, on this nearly empty dance floor, I was Pathetic

Young Girl in Alien Bobble Headband. With deconstructionism, context is everything.

It was only a week or so later that he came to office hours. He was quiet, this young man who sat at the back of class in his uniform of oversize glasses and a hooded sweatshirt.

"So I need to talk to you about something," he began.

I nodded, folding my arms across my baby-doll jumper made from a tablecloth.

"Well, I just wanted to say I don't think I'm going to come to class anymore. The students are out of control, they're not very nice to me, and you don't stop them. I'm not learning anything from you, so I was thinking I'd just skip it. I won't have to deal with you, and you won't have to deal with me. I'll turn in a paper the last week of class, collect my three units, and we'll call it even."

Theoretical formulas I didn't get, but I knew a deal when I saw one. I agreed. I never saw him again, and four months later his paper appeared in my in-box as promised, twelve pages on genetic engineering. As I recall, it was fine but not spectacular, arguing that the rewards outweighed the risks, a simple but clear position supported with evidence, research, quotes. Not stated, but clearly proven, was his thesis that he'd learned more on his own than in my class; though merely fine, his paper was still better than any of his classmates'.

The tendency when grading a paper is to imagine the paper *you* would have written given the same topic. Had this been my paper, I would have moved from my standard dictionary quote opener to comparisons between genetic engineering and literary theory. Genetic engineering, after all, was the scientific discipline where literary theory debates were being played out in test tubes and centrifuges. It was deconstructionism versus essentialism translated into strings of DNA and formulas, charts and probabilities. I would have included a footnote discussing the ways that deconstructionism seems a funny thing when you're twenty-two; how strange, when you're in school trying to find yourself, to find, instead, that there may be no self to find. And if nothing was fixed, why couldn't I be happy in Boston? In grad school? Why couldn't I be well?

Are we nature, or nurture? Do we act on instinct, or learned behavior? Are we shy or brave because of biology or sociology? Did I shake because a genetic mutation compelled me to, or because I'd grown up with it, memorizing the tremor of hands holding salad forks, learning to do the same? Was I a hypochondriac because my brain and body didn't work quite right, or because I enjoyed the show, because there were too many advantages to it to stop?

An essential tremor can have no cause, or it can have many, too many to tease a single one out. I shook because a mechanism in my brain told me to. I shook because I was in the wrong place, doing the wrong thing. I shook because I was uncomfortable in my own skin. I shook because I was nervous, unhappy, overwhelmed. I shook because I was on shaky ground, the tremor a crack in the surface, a fracture over shifting plates.

And so I left. I went back home, back to California to finish an esoteric dissertation I didn't particularly understand. I couldn't follow my own theory, but I think it argued that You Are Here: your identity is determined less by biology or sociology than by geography, which relies on both. I'd grown up in California. Of course I shook. And of course I didn't understand theory. Oh, look, skateboards! Hot dogs are delicious. Let's go to the beach!

I was happier back at home. Even so, the tremors did not go away, and after all this time I don't expect they will. I'm not sure I'd want them to. They've become, in fact, essential, a necessary part of who I am, neurasthenic and nervous, a yappy dog in people clothes. I sometimes get alarmed when I'm *not* shaking, afraid that the stillness indicates an impending stroke or imminent heart attack.

Still, it'd be nice to hold a paper and not make it into a fan.

Now when I have to address a group I take beta-blockers. It's the tiniest little pill you've ever seen, the size of a light-startled pupil, a concentrated magic that erases my tremor entirely and fills my veins with confidence. I don't know how they work. Do they transform me into someone new or let the real me come out, deconstruct or essentialize me, I'm not quite sure. But for six straight hours I am someone else, calm, professional, in charge. I am well and whole: i/n (the)ory.

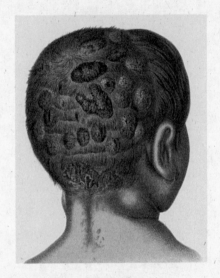

Fig. 10. Impetigo Contagiosa

The Talking Cure

✿

When I finally finished graduate school, my uncle told me I wasn't allowed to use the doctor title, because, he said, "You're not the cutting kind." He had a point. I felt silly using a title I'd earned writing papers about *Gilligan's Island*. I'd hoped people might insist—"Don't be silly, Dr. Traig, you've earned it"—but it never caught on. The only time the title got used was on a card my cousin sent for my graduation, addressed, for reasons I didn't quite understand, to Dr. Ass Clown.

Maybe the name was apt. At the time I was working in a GI lab. I'd failed to find an academic job, but then again, I'd never really tried. The main reason I'd gone to graduate school in the first place was because it left me free to watch daytime talk shows. I was also hoping it might get me on one. In the 1990s there was a staggering number of talk shows, and I figured at least one of them would welcome a topic like "Dr. Traig Tells You How to Dump That Loser" or "Doctor Beauty Secrets." Talk shows always seemed to feature experts whose Ph.D.s turned out to be in esoteric fields like Comp Lit or French. Dr. Laura's Ph.D. is in physiology, which, apparently, is a respectable discipline and not the academic term for PE, but still.

They seemed so much more useful than academic work, these shows. The guests were doing the same thing my classmates and I were—talk, talk, talking—but they were also solving problems. Well, not really. But they were entertaining America, and that was far more than I could say for deconstructionism.

The only thing deconstructionism had taught me was how meaningless titles actually were, something I spent a lot of time thinking about in the all-too-literal-bowels of the gastroenterology department. I was happy enough—I liked the work—but couldn't help feeling I'd gotten off track. "Doctor." I was a Ph.D. who spent her days making photocopies and fielding calls from sigmoidoscope reps. At the hospital my title was "administrative assistant," and while it accurately described what I did, it did not, I felt, sum up who I *was*. What I *was* was a healer, a people person born to serve, a doctor, cutting kind or not, and so it was, a few months after graduation, that I decided to follow my heart and actually start treating people. My hypochondria had come full circle. Now I wasn't just an imaginary invalid; I was an imaginary doctor.

The title I took was "amateur physician." It's apt, I think, though I'll admit that this must be the scariest combination of words in the English language, up there with "rusty thumbtack home acupuncture" and "spray paint anesthesiology." English is the one thing I'm trained in, so I know.

It all began innocently enough and ended messily, like most first cases, starting with a misdiagnosis and concluding in the ER, with more experienced professionals taking charge of the unraveling situation. I'd made a friend dinner, and halfway through the Tater Tots course, it became evident there was a problem. Medical school or no, I can tell when something's wrong, and whimpering and clutching your crotch is an unambiguous clue. Apparently Ryan had been having twinges in his groin region all day, and now it was becoming unignorable. "My testicle feels like it's in a sandwich press," he moaned. "Will you call your dad?"

I would not. I didn't relish the thought of discussing anyone's balls with my father, but more than that, it had occurred to me that this was an opportunity to have my very own patient, my first, and I wasn't eager to hand over the reins. Instead I suggested we ice his crotch with the bottle of Colt 45 we were using to wash down our dinner.

"I think it's getting worse," he gasped, half an hour later.

"Maybe the Colt would work better if you just drank it."

When that failed, I wondered if we should puncture the organ in question. "You know, to relieve some of the pressure."

"We're not microwaving hot dogs here!"

"Let's try it."

"Call. Your. Dad."

And so ensued the most uncomfortable conversation my father and I have ever shared. The term "testicular torsion" was used—another scary pair of words—along with the phrase "Seek medical attention or he'll lose a nut." In short order we were on our way to a hospital, where our vocabularies were expanded to include the terms "bell clapper deformity" (here I pictured deformed band members) and "tunica vaginalis" (a crotchless ethnic garment), both of which actually turn out to refer to urological phenomena. The professionals took over and I spent the rest of the night in the waiting room, doing something I'm actually good at, watching talk shows. And it occurred to me, sitting there, watching Maury help a young girl identify her baby's daddy, that, I, too, was helping people, and I was helping people using Maury's tools: talk. I'd botched the case, sure, but now Ryan was getting the care he needed, and it was, in part, because of the conversation with my father. I had, in a way, effected a talking cure.

It was incredibly satisfying. Treating people made me feel important and needed, so I was delighted when my second case came along soon after. This time it was a bout of giardia, an intestinal parasite also known as beaver fever. Fittingly, the victim had picked it up at a lesbian retreat. I misdiagnosed this one, too, but I was right for the three cases that followed, correctly diagnosing friends' scabies, impetigo, and bleeding hemorrhoids. I was wrong with the lead poisoning, but right with the fibroids and endometriosis. I correctly diagnosed one friend's Asperger's syndrome and yet another friend's borderline personality disorder, though, it should be pointed out, both strongly dispute my findings and an actual licensed therapist has yet to back me up. Still: have lunch with either one of them and just tell me I'm wrong.

I do, in fact, have about twenty years of medical experience, having worked in medical offices most of my adult life. And while I never got the chance to interact with patients, the ample downtime did allow plenty of opportunities to interact with WebMD. Researching my own imaginary illnesses, I learned about every single way to get sick, and every kind of treatment.

My own treatment methods mostly involve words, talking, telling stories. You'd be amazed what you can solve with just a short chat. Just the other day a friend called, complaining of bloody diarrhea. She's young and healthy, but she sometimes gets stomachaches, and she has a history of anal fissures. We have the kind of friendship that permits me to ask if she's been wiping too hard, but in this case the answer was no. We were briefly stumped. But talk of bloody diarrhea naturally led to talk of food, which prompted her to rave about a root salad she'd eaten the previous day. Eureka. The medical mystery was solved, all via phone: not blood, but beets.

Sometimes I'm more hands-on, prescribing treatments or tinctures. Because I don't have a DEA license, my pharmacy is limited mostly to alcohol and lotions. You can scoff, but from what I understand that's the sum total of French medical practice.

Mostly, however, I just use words. Literature was, in its way, great training, as were the talk shows that had made me want to go to graduate school in the first place. People in books and on TV get sick all the time; they need to, for our entertainment. Usually they get the disease they deserve, which is why poetic justice is a big part of my practice. This is how I know the woman who took the last box of ice cream sandwiches even though I was clearly reaching for it has hepatitis, while the nice person who let me cut in line because I only had one thing doesn't need to worry about that mole; it's benign. My exams aren't physical, but metaphysical, often consisting of a single question: what do you have coming to you? Sometimes, of course, you get the last thing you deserve (case in point: my recent bout of *jock itch*), which is why I also consider the literary technique of irony. Dramatic tension is also a factor. The diagnosis has to make narrative sense. The lump in your breast can only be cancer if you're planning your wedding, or are newly pregnant; if, in short, it's sweeps in the soap opera of your life.

For me, nothing is more fascinating. I have always loved medical stories best. As a child, my favorite bedtime stories were my mother's anecdotes from nursing school, and I begged her to repeat them over and over. "Tell me again about the time you took a sheep's eye from the lab and left it in your roommate's sock drawer," I implored. "Tell me about the patient who smeared feces on the wall." I devoured her issues of *Good Housekeeping*, looking for tragic articles about toddlers with cystic fibrosis and the heartbreak of Tay-Sachs. I loved the movies, too, the after-school specials about teens battling leukemia, the movie of the week about a very special diabetic boy whose parents won't let him lose his legs.

It's utterly compelling even though there's no suspense. We know exactly how it's going to turn out. The medical story always follows a formula. Everything's fine, then all of a sudden the puzzling symptom appears. The odd lump, the clump of hair in the brush, the unexplained falls: the audience can diagnose these as well as any doctor can. As soon as the heroine finds the unwelcome mass in her armpit, we know what's coming. In real life, doctors often refer to the "scrip"—it's short for prescription, but there is a script in all these stories, and there's a script, of a kind, in medical practice too, lines you run, a well-rehearsed scene you play out again and again. When this symptom presents, you run this test, and you make that diagnosis. I know what's coming, but I never get tired of it.

Part of the reason I liked working in medical offices was that I got great stories every single day. The best stories came from a stint answering phones at an HMO. The HMO's name had the banal vagueness typical of government agencies, and for this reason it was frequently mistaken for the Department of Health. All day long I received calls from the sick and irate, too angry or disoriented to look up the right number, but well enough to talk.

"I'd like to report the popcorn shop out at the mall," one elderly woman complained. "The caramel corn gave my husband and me gas like you wouldn't believe. Gas and the dipsy doodles. We were leaping over each other to get to the toilet."

"There's a pile of bloody trash in front of my house," reported another. "I'm serious. There's, like, a year's worth of used tampons. I can't imagine where it came from, but you guys might want to come haul it away before the dogs get to it."

I'd spent years studying the world's greatest literature and I'd never gotten stories like these. Because my father actually takes confidentiality seriously, I was denied these growing up. This had been agonizing to a child like me, who loved a good medical story, and I'd often spent mealtimes badgering him for information.

"You have to tell me what you're treating my geography teacher for. Now, I already know she's your patient because she told me. You might as well just spill."

"I'm not telling you anything."

"Is that because it's a weird sex thing?"

"I'm not going to answer that."

"Will you at least tell me if she's a hermaphrodite?"

When this failed, I'd try to trick him by pretending I already knew the gist of it. "Mrs. Ferguson said to tell you her colon has never felt so good," I might begin. "But she wanted me to ask you how often she should be changing her colostomy bag. You can just let me know, you know, whatever information she might need about her colostomy bag, and I'll just give her the message tomorrow in class."

When I began working in medical offices myself, I realized the stories are only good if you don't know the patient, the talk only satisfying when you don't really care. At my first medical job, that tentative summer in the basement of my father's clinic, I'd expected gossip to be one of the perks. It was the only clinic in town, and that room contained all the secrets of everyone I'd ever met. But when I had to open the files of someone I knew, a neighbor or a friend's parent, it made me so profoundly uncomfortable I'd will myself to forget whatever I'd just seen. It's the opposite of books and movies; you can only enjoy the story if you're not invested in the character. If you do, the missing testicle is more painful than funny, the bowel impaction more tragic than amusing.

When you don't know the person, though, when it's an anonymous caller, or an unlucky young mother in a magazine: totally absorbing. Everybody loves a good cancer story, a juicy lupus diary. I'm not sure why. I think we tell ourselves it's so we'll be able to recognize the symptoms should we get them ourselves, or that it's because we're too compassionate to turn the page and leave the story of suffering unread. But we know that's not really true. It's not a gesture of support or community; it's a distancing, a vicarious tour through hell in which what matters is that it's happening to you: not me. It's an incision, a break. It's a verbal vaccination. We read them to say: no, no, I don't have a lump in my abdomen. I don't have a skull-crushing, brain-tumorous headache. No, no: that won't happen to me. Of course, if you're a hypochondriac, it probably will.

You need to sever yourself from the story to tolerate it, most especially when it's real. I suppose that's why the literature of daily medical practice, the charting and the reports, is so impersonal. "Clinical" has become synonymous with detachment. This is the cutting kind of writing, surgically precise, cut off.

Medical language facilitates a certain separation. It has to, or you couldn't do this every day. It's something I'm used to. In our house things were always called by their clinical names. When asked on our preschool application what we called our private parts and bathroom terms, our responses were matter-of-fact: perineum and voiding. My parents tolerated a certain amount of baby talk—hot dogs were jut-juts, but penises were never wieners.

The problem, of course, is that words can't be controlled much better than preschoolers can. Confusions persist. I was often baffled by the reports that crossed my desk. Due to the nursing shortage, many nurses come from abroad, and while their clinical skills are fine their English can be bumpy. "His butt got stucked to that commode," wrote one, explaining how a patient had gotten a laceration. "Mrs. Patty in 707, she have the lices," said another.

Then, of course, there are the doctors, with their famously illegible penmanship. I'm not sure it's worse than anyone else's, but the stakes are certainly higher. When the difference between R EAR and REAR is whether your ointment goes into your right ear or your rectum, you hope the writing's clear.

And here is where medicine deviates from literature, where the stories diverge. Literature wants words to have an infinite number or meanings; medicine wants just one. Medicine asks you to write as unambiguously as possible. It demands a surgical precision. For this reason medicine frowns on homonyms, on double meanings and gray areas. There are rules, a medical grammar of sorts. A lot of the rules concern abbreviations. Some are permitted; others are not. SOB is fine (shortness of breath), as are HO (house officer) and NAD (no apparent distress), but MS is banned because it can mean too many things: multiple sclerosis or morphine sulfate or magnesium sulfate. QID is out, but DIC and F/U are perfectly fine. FUC (fucosidase), FUCA (alpha-L-fucosidase), HOMO (highest occupied molecular orbital), even Gas Anal F & T (gastric analysis, free and total)—in medicine, these are all completely acceptable.

For many years it was my job to make sure these rules were followed. When things went awry, I got a report, which I wrote up and filed away. It was always tempting to edit it, to perform verbal surgery, to rewrite the ending and make the patient someone who had their illness coming. I wanted to make a tidy report, a narrative that made sense. Because usually it doesn't; it's terrifyingly random. And sometimes it seems deliberately, cruelly unfair: the baby dies, while the drug-dealing rapist lives.

A year or so after I left graduate school, the man who'd been my closest friend there was diagnosed with lymphoma. By then we'd drifted apart somewhat. I'd moved across the country, and I was too busy with my talk shows to talk. Besides, it was his turn to contact me.

"What, were your hands broken?" I huffed, when finally, he called.

Not broken, but wired to IV poles. I am used to feeling like a jerk, but never had I stepped in it like this. He was really sick. It was a terrible lymphoma, he explained, aggressive and fast. This was not amateur medicine, but advanced, stage IV, beyond all hope.

Over the next few months I tried, like an asshole, to treat

it with words. I sent him sunny cards and optimistic books, big glossy hardbacks written by scrappy cancer survivors that, had I been within striking distance, he would have been perfectly justified in using to club me. I called and delivered pep talks. "Some positive thinking, that's what you need," I chirped. "I want you to picture the white blood cells just gobbling that bad old cancer up." A macrobiotic diet. A feng shui makeover. Acupuncture. Alcohol and lotions. Surely there was a cure. He wasn't even thirty yet, was not at the high point of his career or his personal life, had hardly even begun. It didn't make narrative sense for him to die now, with the plot all unfolded.

In cancer stories, the friend is normally played by a well-groomed, well-funded effortless beauty who steps in to treat the dying patient to the high life as life is ending. She arranges visits from movie stars, shopping sprees, trips to Walt Disney World with oxygen tank in tow. I was not she, and he was not the brave cinematic martyr. He was angry and bitter, and I was sheepish and guilty. Hypochondriacs are great with terminal illness when it's imaginary and happening to them, terrible when it's real and happening to others.

Another's illness may, in fact, be the only thing that causes a hypochondriac shame. Most of us will happily drop our pants for a completely unnecessary endoscopy, then send the bill to our insurance company without a moment's embarrassment or guilt. But another's illness makes us cringe, like we're the Germans at the Holocaust remembrance service.

I didn't know what to say. It became hard to have a conversation with him. It wasn't even: I'd complain about my dates;

he'd complain about having chemo drugs poured into a shunt in his skull. A *shunt* in his *skull*—no, *that's* the scariest pair of words in the English language.

He died the weekend of the Academy Awards. We were both big fans of spectacles and pageantry, so I'd called that morning to wish him happy Oscar Sunday. I left a message on his machine, not realizing he'd already passed, and it made me unspeakably depressed to think about the friend or family member who'd erase it, pack up the machine, and donate it to some thrift store where his outgoing message would sit dormant on the shelf of a shop he wouldn't have been caught dead in, except that he was.

That year, as in most, the favorite for Best Actor had been nominated for portraying the victim of a terrible disease, and watching him give his speech, I found myself, for the first time in a while, speechless. I'd see the movie a few years later, and think about my friend, as I watched this healthy man, playing sick. I'd think about myself, playing doctor, and the relief we share in knowing it's just a role. No, no: it won't happen to me, we can tell ourselves, it's just a story, and at any moment, the director will yell "Cut!"

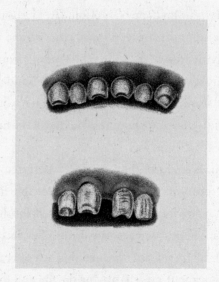

Fig. 11. Syphilitic Teeth

Wisdom Teeth

✿

Descended from leprechauns on one side and trolls on the other, I am not what you'd call a genetic lottery winner. Kinky hair, stumpy legs, a waist so short it is sometimes mistaken for an unusually thick neck—this is my lot. Over the years I have grown to accept it, and I no longer resent the lucky relatives who've escaped my fate, making off with all the willowy recessive genes and leaving me the squat, frizzy genetic detritus. I don't begrudge the long-legged aunts, the slim cousins, with their smooth manes and natural highlights. I am what I am, and I don't much mind, except for the teeth. The *teeth*. In every sense of the word except the traditional one, my teeth bite.

This is the family legacy. My great-aunts used to say we were descended from royalty, and I suspect it's because our ancestors had mouths full of crowns. Most of my family members have terrible teeth, and my parents have the worst of the lot. Lacking dental insurance, they are now in the process of slowly transferring the contents of their retirement accounts to a variety of dental specialists. Every month there is a new -dontist: the endodontist and the prosthodontist, the orthodontist and the periodontist, a constant parade of new experts my parents need as fast as they can invent them.

My mother's teeth are so notoriously flinty that the family now places bets on which tooth my mother will break on which day, eating which food. If you picked front tooth, July 1, 2004, Chinese chicken salad, you would have cleaned up. For weeks afterward she delighted us all with her Granny Clampett routine. She acquired a replacement which she wears when she goes out, but at home, she prefers a more natural hillbilly look. She says she likes being able to push food through the space, allowing her to eat without doing all the hard work of actually opening her mouth. "Plus," she says, "it makes it easier to play my jug."

The apple did not fall far from the tree, which means that I, too, must eat mine cored and baked. I'm fairly certain my teeth are made of papier-mâché. Most people would panic if a molar crumbled upon biting into pudding, but for me that's a fairly common occurrence. I've broken teeth on tofu, dental floss, and tomato soup. I've gotten used to dentists shaking their heads and sighing when I open my mouth. Every few months I need to have some excruciating new procedure performed. It becomes routine. I settle into the chair, blink at the great plumes of smoke coming out of my mouth, swallow the burnt-hair taste, then write an enormous check and agree that we must get together and do this again soon.

We must. I like my dentist because he tells me things like,

"You know, dentistry is really a very crude science." He's right, but it was once cruder still. The history of dentistry is an appalling business, an absolute shitstorm of malpractice and agony, disinformation and lunacy. What fascinates me are the transhistorical, cross-cultural consistencies. I'm amazed that so many different cultures had the same bad ideas. Both the Romans and the French favored urine mouthwash. Romans and Germans believed toothaches could be relieved by transferring them to trees. And until the Middle Ages, nearly every culture, even ones that had no contact with each other, blamed toothaches on "tooth worms." Worms got in your teeth through food or spontaneous generation, it was believed, and when they were restless caused toothaches. This universally held misapprehension may be due to the fact that the pulp, the live bit of flesh at the center of a tooth, does look a little like a curled-up worm. In any case, the result was that for the better part of history, dentistry was less medicine than pest control. Fumigation was the preferred treatment. Early dentists treated toothaches by smoking them with the herb henbane. This did nothing for the infection but got you high enough not to care, and produced wormy ashes that seemed proof of the critters' demise.

When bugs weren't being rooted out they were being applied. Leeching and bloodletting were also popular techniques, becoming standard dental treatments by the time of George Washington, whose terrible teeth required constant care. Bloodletting was, in fact, the treatment that killed him. He survived the Potomac only to succumb to a sore throat after doctors relieved him of five pints. I bet he didn't even get a doughnut. And even if he had, he couldn't have chewed it.

Despite their reputation, English teeth weren't particularly bad until refined sugar became widely available. The English took to it with gusto—they sugared their *meat* dishes—and by the Elizabethan age blackened teeth were the rule, each mouth a swampy wetland of decay. The swampiest probably belonged to Elizabeth herself, rumored to have had a terrible sweet tooth. By the end of her life, even that tooth had to be removed. She'd already lost her hair due to lead poisoning from the makeup she'd used to cover up her smallpox scars, so the once-great beauty took to padding her cheeks with wads of cotton, Marlon Brando in a spangly red wig.

Josephine Bonaparte fared better in the looks department but just as poorly in the dental. She had the dark, diseased teeth you'd expect from a woman raised on a sugar plantation. They were so bad she took to hiding them demurely behind a handkerchief, a shocking practice in itself. At the time, handkerchiefs were considered too vulgar to be used in mixed company, so this was a little like dabbing one's mouth with soiled underpants. In time the shock wore off and the trend caught on. And in any case, we can presume her husband—who is rumored to have written her, "I'll be home in three days. Don't bathe"—didn't much mind.

The worst American teeth probably belonged to poor George Washington, who was plagued by painful dental rot and gum disease until his unfortunate end. Tooth loss and bad partials made it difficult to speak. If he could not tell a lie, it was because it was hard for him to say much of anything. By middle age he'd lost all his teeth (the last one was gilded and enshrined at the New York Academy of Medicine, where it remains on display today). The dentures that followed proved even worse. At the time, dentures were spring-loaded, forcing the mouth open in a chronic Pac-Man position; to keep his mouth shut, Washington had to clench his jaw at all times. Contrary to legend, the dentures were made not of wood but of hippo tusk. Washington also had a set made from elk and cow choppers, which raises the possibility that he chewed a roast *with its own teeth*.

But it couldn't be helped. American dentistry didn't really get off the ground until the formation of the Baltimore College of Dental Surgery in 1839, and even this was a bit of a rocky start. One of its founders, Solymon Brown, was also a poet, and took it upon himself to compose a five-canto epic on the subject of dentistry that is generally acknowledged to be one of the worst poems of all time. Behold, a taste of "Dentologia":

For, as the witching music of the lyre,
Is heard along each vibratory wire,
What time the heaven-instructed minstrel flings
His hurried hand among the magic strings:—
So when disease invades the dental arch,
And strides in anguish on his angry march,
His burning touch, like the electric flame,
Finishes through every fibre of the frame;

Fever ensues, with all its raging fires,

And oft the maniac sufferer expires.

And yet of all the evils that accrue

From loss of teeth through neither small nor few;

The chief is this;—'tis nature's general plan,

That all the solid aliments of man,

Before admission to the secret divine,

Transforms the cruder mass to milky chime,

By nature's metamorphosis sublime,—

Should suffer comminution:—hence we find

The dental organs formed to cut, and grind,

And masticate the food:—this rightly done,

The process of digestion, well begun,

results in health to each dependent part,

That feels the living impulse of the heart.

But when, from loss of teeth, the food must pass,

A crude, and rigid, and unbroken mass.

To the digestive organs: who can know,

What various forms of complicated woe,

May rise terrific from that single source?

For nature, once resisted in her course,

Breeds frightful things—a monstrous progeny!

Consumption, fevers, palsy, leprosy,

The hobbling gout, that chides, at every breath,

The lingering pace of all-destroying death;

And apoplexy, dragging to his doom
The half surviving victim to the tomb.

The poem laments the tragedies that befall a young lady who neglects her teeth, a lesson I ought to heed. I'm willing to admit I have some of my dental karma coming. There was a ten-year period when I didn't go to the dentist at all. I drink unthinkable amounts of tooth-dissolving sodas. I floss only when compelled by the threat of gum surgery. I sometimes substitute Mountain Dew for mouthwash, on the grounds that it is the same color and, I figure, acidic enough to kill things. I don't brush properly. I don't Waterpik. I don't Sonicare. I don't massage my gums; I am sickened by the thought. My entire dental care routine takes thirty seconds a day. I spend more time putting on tights.

My sister's dental habits are even worse. To my knowledge, she has flossed her teeth only once, and that was done purely to gross me out, at dinner, using a strand of my own hair. So it does not seem fair that despite this and our shared DNA, she has extraordinary teeth. Who knows where she gets them from. Hygienists are awestruck by their blindingly white hue, their cavity-free indestructibility. At her last appointment the entire office staff abandoned their own patients mid cleaning to marvel at Vicky's thirty-two gleaming Chiclets.

"So you say these aren't veneers? And you've never had your teeth whitened?"

"Nope, and I bathe them daily in coffee and red wine."

The hygienists shook their heads in disbelief. "They're like snow."

Mine are more like yellow snow. When I was seventeen, having never touched tobacco or even tea, the dental assistant asked how many packs I went through a day. "Might as well start smoking, then," my mother replied when I told her. "Especially if you're thinking about getting pregnant anytime soon. Low birth weight makes for a *much* easier delivery. You'll thank me."

Might as well. Teeth talk. They're a record of the choices you've made. My teeth apparently lied, but it wasn't long before I'd taken on the bad dental habits that my teeth were already indicating. Why floss when gum disease was a genetic inevitability? Why not guzzle coffee when they're already light tan? Teeth reveal the essential self. They are the ultimate identifier, the part they will know you by when the rest of your body rots away. Five hundred years from now anthropologists can look at your jaw and know exactly how you lived your life. Mine will show that snack cakes were a twentieth-century staple food.

Bad teeth are my fate. Personally, I'm inclined to blame the tooth fairy. As a young child I'd adored her. Unlike the dentist, she rewarded me when teeth fell out of my mouth. This was splendid, and established a system of compensating bad behavior that would hinder me the rest of my life.

At four I began to prefer the tooth fairy to my mother for the simple reason that she was more likely to wear chiffon. That she was, in fact, my mother in a nightgown never occurred to me. On nights I expected a visit from her I slept as I did on nights I feared burglars, my mouth fixed in an angelic smile that I hoped would arouse mercy and affection.

For the next several years I was fairly obsessed. I'd imagine what she'd do with the teeth, what she did for money, how she spent her free time.

"I bet she cleans her bathroom," my mother said, pulling on a pair of rubber gloves. This seemed like a loaded statement, a hint, but just what was she suggesting? It was impossible that the tooth fairy was the same woman I saw before me, her entire forearm in the toilet, trying to fish out the hairbrush I'd flushed in a moment of boredom.

The tooth fairy cleaning the bathroom? What did she know? Me, I'd seen the tooth fairy on several occasions, a gauzy and benevolent twilight visitor, and had come to think of her as an intimate acquaintance. I spoke of her often, gratuitously working a mention into any conversation. Friends and family rolled their eyes at my endless name-dropping. Homework, TV, dinner menus—I'd mention her no matter what the topic. "So, the tooth fairy? She visits me, like a lot? Even when I don't lose a tooth? I guess you could say we're friends. Anyway, I bet she likes pizza."

After a few years of this my mother got sick of it and announced there'd been a staffing change in the tooth fairy office. The nameless Disney-esque sprite I was so fond of had been replaced, she said, by a friendly homosexual named Bruce. It was around this time I began to suspect my mother was behind the whole operation, a hunch confirmed when I found a ziplock bag of milk teeth in my mother's nightstand. Still, I continued to write the tooth fairy letters because Bruce was such a charming correspondent. "What do you think of the new Olivia Newton-John album?" he'd ask. "I think she should stick to ballads, but that's just me." He'd politely inquire about our lives, and then catch us up on his own. "I'm thinking of getting a Maltese," he'd write. "They're high-strung, but they don't shed, and with my suede furniture, that's a real concern." When we stopped losing teeth Bruce continued to write us once a year, on Christmas Eve, leaving his note next to Santa's. After all these years he'd become a close friend; of course we'd exchange holiday cards.

So it didn't surprise anyone when, many years later, I moved in with a brace of Bruces. My friendship with the tooth fairy did not leave me with good dental care habits, but it did make me an enormous fag hag, and when it was time to live on my own, naturally, I chose to do it with homosexuals. I moved to the Castro and set up house with a gay cousin and two gay friends. Now, when I was awakened in the middle of the night, it was not by a fairy in a chiffon nightgown, but by a fairy in cargo pants, someone's brand-new boyfriend trying to find his way to the bathroom in the dark. They did not leave change under my pillows, but after a particularly vigorous makeout session some of it might end up under my couch cushions, and I was happy to harvest the proceeds however they came.

At the time I was trying very hard to model myself on Dorothy Parker. It's such a cliché, the aspiration of every gay or girl who doesn't get asked out in high school. We'd be better off copying Truman Capote. Him, at least, I looked something like. But Dorothy Parker was my muse, and so I did my dead best to imitate her. I knew "friend of Dorothy" meant something else, but still, a coterie of homosexual admirers seemed like the sort of accessory one might need for this endeavor, like a smart suit jacket or an engraved hip flask. They would compliment my droll wit, call me an exquisite creature, assure me that they'd marry me if only they were straight.

The reality was a little less rosy. Unlike Bruce, my roommates would not reward me for lapses in hygiene or social graces. They tended to say things like, "You can't leave the house in that." "You are the dirtiest girl I've ever met. Not dirty like saucy. Dirty like unwashed." "I was going to do your laundry for you, but when I saw the state of your things I thought I'd be doing you a bigger favor to throw them away, which is exactly what I did."

They were right, though. Sloppy and inclined to snack, I was less Dorothy Parker than Dorothy Porker, less Algonquin Round Table than Round Table Pizza. "The first thing I do in the morning is brush my teeth and sharpen my tongue," Dorothy Parker wrote. I usually ate some mint chip ice cream and went back to bed.

It was a pale imitation, but at least I dressed the part. Cocktail Nation was in full swing, and by happy hour I'd be all dolled up in peplums and pencil skirts, ready for drunken repartee. My roommates and I favored a subterranean, red-lit, velvet-swathed former speakeasy, less because of its Algonquinian overtones than its two-dollar drinks, and went there so often that the bartender would start to mix my Manhattan as soon as he saw my ankles on the top stair. I showed up dutifully every afternoon, downing drinks and waiting for the witty aphorisms to start popping out of my mouth.

I don't remember any of that happening. Here's what I do remember:

- Dumping an ashtray into my roommate's coat pocket because he wasn't paying enough attention to me.
- Finishing strangers' drinks when they went to the bathroom.
- Borrowing a promotional marquee from Kentucky Fried Chicken and dragging it up to my apartment, where, for the next two weeks, it informed visitors that my breasts were both spicy and priced to move.
- Crashing strangers' parties, helping myself to their birthday presents, then criticizing the hosts loudly and *in French* when they asked me to leave, thus proving that it is in fact possible to be pretentious and totally classless at the exact same time.

The end result of all this was a lot of people started thinking I was a jackass. Also, my teeth got messed up. Maybe it was from trying so hard to be mordant and biting, or maybe it was from too many acidic gimlets. Perhaps I wore the enamel off vomiting margaritas and opening screw-tops with my teeth. Or maybe it was because I didn't floss and rarely managed to brush before sleep seized me on the living room floor where, the next morning, I would awake, fuzzy-toothed and cotton-mouthed, with "Bi-otch!!" written in lipstick on my forehead. This was not the witty literary exchange I'd expected. When Dorothy Parker passed out, Robert Benchley didn't vandalize her, did he?

One morning I noticed a molar had turned a deep charcoal gray. How had this happened? I'd known other people with discolored teeth, but they'd always had a story. They'd fallen face-first into a tree, or grown up in Russia. Maybe they'd had a mishap on the basketball court, or lost the tooth in a fight. The story always ended with them rushing to the ER with the tooth in a cup of milk, only to have it die after replantation. But my gray tooth just showed up. Sure, I hadn't seen the inside of a dentist's office in seven or eight years, but still—a gray tooth? That seemed like the sort of thing that occurred only after a long time on a strict Appalachian dental care regime of brushing your teeth with cake frosting and gargling with chaw, which, come to think of it, is more or less what I did.

The gray tooth was a wake-up call. I'd managed to ignore the skin damage and the alienated friends, but here was concrete proof that my lifestyle was getting me nowhere; and that, in any case, I needed to be a teensy bit more responsible because, please, a gray tooth. Clearly, I had to do something about this *right away*, no *really*, and two years later I managed to make an appointment to get it fixed.

Hoping the bill might go to my parents, I went to their dentist. This was the same dental office I'd gone to as a child. Now it was run by my dentist's son, who, evidently, had made much better use of his twenties than I had. He had a staff, malpractice insurance and a benefit plan, an office suite with a terrarium. He was only a couple years older than I was, but he was so much more *responsible*. I couldn't be trusted to brush my own teeth.

Hence, the gray tooth. Hence, also, the X-rays that revealed eight cavities. Hence the rest of the day was spent staring at acoustic tile as a series of picks and drills chipped away at my will to live. Getting all the decay cleaned out and filled in took hours. The staff had to bring in backup. By the time it was over I felt and looked very much like I'd been beat up, and as I walked home, cars slowed to point at the girl stomping home in the heat with her face leaking drool.

I was nearly thirty so I can't explain what I was wearing, dressed like a member of Blink-182, in a faded black T-shirt and those short pants that I believe are called "surfer jams," designed to show off calf tattoos. You'd think the gays could have straightened me out in that department a little.

When I was halfway home the dentist drove by. He pulled over, still in his suit, and rolled down the window of his sports car. I could feel the air-conditioning on my face. "You want a ride?" he asked.

It was kind of him to offer. But to accept somehow meant acknowledging all my failures: I was thirty, incapable of driving myself, incapable of any adult activity, really. Incapable of *brushing.* It seemed better to pretend I was walking because I *wanted* to.

"No fanks."

"It's a hundred degrees out here."

"I wike walking."

"You're sure?"

"Yef."

"Suit yourself." He shrugged. Then he smiled, revealing straight white teeth, and drove off with a friendly wave.

Because I was too sore to eat and there was nothing else to do, I spent the rest of the day taking stock of my life. How had I gotten here? I dressed like a bike messenger or an extra from *Swing Kids*. I'd found all my furniture off the street, and some of the time, I think, I wasn't recycling so much as outright stealing. I was drunk half the time. I treated my friends like crap. I had, I realized, been acting like a jerk for ten years—which was around the last time I'd been to the dentist, in fact.

That visit had been to remove my wisdom teeth. The name has always struck me as a little odd. Cultures tend to link the loss of teeth with diminished vitality, or even vision, but not intelligence. And having your wisdom teeth removed doesn't relieve you of any brain cells, though the nitrous oxide might. Still, it's hard not to make the connection. Wisdom teeth come and go at a time when you've got the body and the rights of an adult but the mind of a preteen, making the bad decisions typical of a former child star. Ask anyone for the story of their wisdom teeth extraction and you'll find it invariably involves a bong, a bar fight, and oral sex before the stitches are even out.

Wisdom teeth are a vestigial organ, a useless evolutionary remnant. At one time they were needed to replace the teeth

lost and broken cracking walnuts or towing crude farm ma-
chinery. The modern lifestyle is easier on molars, so wisdom
teeth usually come into a mouth with no occupancy, and have
to be removed.

Ten years after mine had come out, it was time to wise up.
I'd gotten too long in the tooth for this lifestyle, and something had to change. Over the next few months I abandoned
the Dorothy Parker routine, gave away my cocktail shaker, upgraded my cable, and retreated to my bedroom. I bought a can
of Comet. I made a salad every once in a while. I would like to
report I passed through the next few years with a sage grace,
with wisdom and maturity. In fact it was more of the same,
with less vomiting and more floss.

My roommates told me it was my Saturn return, the two-
year period at the end of your twenties when Saturn returns to
the position it was on your natal chart, causing chaotic changes
and mood swings. I'm not sure I believe in astrology, but I do
believe in assholes, and over the next six months I became a
four-star one. Bruce once left me notes. Now I left them for
my roommates, passive-aggressive commentaries blaming
them for everything that was wrong with my life. "I don't know
who left the crime scene in the bathtub, but please clean it
up." "Will the responsible party kindly deal with the City of
Night on the third shelf of the refrigerator?" "The next time
you decide to shower drunk, please don't blow your nose on
my loofah." Or, simply, "SHITPIGS."

My roommates, thoughtfully, did not retaliate in kind, a
note for a note, a tooth for a tooth, but instead, realizing the

only way we'd continue to love one another is if we didn't live with one another, found other places to live. I punished them for this betrayal for a couple years, then realized they were right.

Dentistry deals with problems by getting to the root of them. The rest of life is more complicated. Removing the rot takes years, not hours; veneers can't conceal the crooked parts. Gradually, however, my life aligned and cleaned up. My neighbors stopped hating me. I started paying my own bills. I stopped trying to be the only girl at the roundtable, the fag hag at the circuit party. I still see my Bruces, but now, instead of tea dances, we just meet over tea. I still get a couple cavities a year, but I don't wake up with graffiti on my forehead. I don't make snarky comments about my friends and call it wit. I mean, I make them, but I don't call it wit.

As for the gray tooth, even after it was cleaned out and filled, it remained gray. Someday maybe I'll get a veneer put on it. But it's not too noticeable if I don't open too wide, so for now, mostly, I just try to keep my mouth shut.

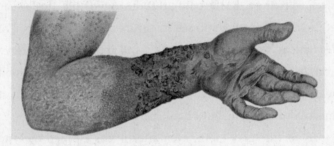

Fig. 12. Eczema

Flesh and Blood

✣

Eventually, however, you have to open your mouth to breathe or eat or drink six margaritas. I celebrated my thirtieth birthday, like my first, by throwing up on myself, and I don't remember either one. If the pictures are any indication that first one was a better party, a humdinger wasted on someone too young to enjoy a mixed drink. In the background you can see the guests, tanned in their Lilly Pulitzer shifts and madras shorts, laughing over Kent Filters as they rest their highballs on speakers the size of small refrigerators piping Brazilian jazz. I appear slightly dazed, nesting in a pile of torn wrapping paper and gifts. By the look of things I've made out pretty well. There's a toddler-size tricycle and a toy piano, some blankets and stuffed animals. But the most significant present is evident on my face, legs, and arms: the flaming full-body rash that had shown up the week before.

My mother had given me her eczema. I suppose it was a genetic bequest she had no control over, but it seemed more like a transfer, like she had, in fact, given me *her* eczema. She'd been plagued with it all her life, but when she got pregnant it went away and never came back.

Not on her body, anyway. By that first birthday it was all over mine. Rashes aren't unusual for babies, who generally spend a lot of time smeared in their own pore-clogging filth, but it quickly became clear this wasn't one of the typical infant conditions. Had I been wearing my diaper on my face, it might have made sense, but *this*—it was unreasonable. My whole head was red and lumpy, a bucket of buffalo wings in an eyelet dress.

The culprit was a mutation sprinkled somewhere on chromosomes 1, 3, 13, 15, 17, and 20. It's a genetic defect that runs thickly in my bloodline, plaguing innumerable cousins and aunts. This is our inheritance. Our hands are adorned not with heirloom rings but pus-filled vesicles and scabs. The family jewel is a carbuncle.

For reasons that aren't entirely clear, the mutation that causes eczema is nearly always partnered with asthma and hay fever. My mother had the complete set. In her children, the lot was split; I got the eczema, and, a short time later, my sister arrived with the rest of the package, the genetic aberration sliced neatly in two like we were sharing a cupcake.

As far as I was concerned there was no question who'd gotten the better deal. Vicky could sit out during PE, and I wasn't allowed to have chocolate. It didn't seem like an even trade. Sure, asthma was far more debilitating and potentially life-threatening, but with greater risk comes greater payoff. Asthma was something you overcame to win Olympic medals. Eczema was something you applied ointment to.

It wasn't fair. Straight hair, long legs—she even got the better *disease.* "It all evens out," our parents liked to say, but that's because they weren't actually keeping score. The pictures from that first birthday reveal that my mother is amply pregnant already, and I sometimes think it was the stress of this impending trauma that brought my eczema out in the first place. From the moment Vicky was born, I was preoccupied with *getting mine.* She was too, and for the rest of our lives every single transaction would be monitored. Who got to ride in front and who languished in the way-back, whose sandwich was made on the heel of the loaf and who got the crusts cut off: it would all go into the running calculations of Who They Loved More, to be tallied when we died and inscribed on our headstones.

Perhaps because of the eczema, I've always had this, itchy fingers, a grasping need to claim things as my own. Realizing everything would be divided between the two of us for the rest of our lives, and that we were likely to outlive our parents, I started calling dibs on family possessions at an alarmingly early age. "Can I have this when you die?" was one of my first full sentences. My sister had already inherited the better genetic mutation; it seemed smart to claim what I could early on. I was particularly interested in my mother's foundation garments and checkbook, but everything was subject to my claims: the patch of carpet with the best view of the TV, the one dinner plate without a chip, the corner piece of cake, the privilege of pushing the elevator button, the Atari, the Rubik's Cube, the dog's love—it was all rightfully mine, and I had no intention of sharing it.

My parents were quick to figure out that they would have to buy two of everything, but still, there were things that were hard to divide evenly, like attention and love and pudding, and there was always something to fight over. We squabbled constantly: Itchy & Scratchy. I suppose the eczema was almost fitting, but it was also redundant. It seemed pointless to scratch myself when my sister already was, taking a long-nailed swipe at me whenever I walked by.

Her asthma was redundant, too, in that I sometimes tried to smother her, but still, it was the better malady. There's no poetry in eczema. It's the disease of the nerd, the wimp, partnered in the imagination with taped glasses and orthopedic shoes. Alice Cooper had it, which is sort of cool, but he knew better than to sing power ballads about it. The closest thing there is to an eczema martyr is Jean-Paul Marat, the French revolutionary, who was stabbed to death while soaking in a tepid tub to soothe a flare-up—not a particularly noble way to go.

Eczema is a disease of the overly sensitive, the hysterical. That's how it works, in fact. Eczema sufferers have both unusually permeable skin and a frantic immune system. We make abnormally high levels of an immunoglobulin called IgE, which is the drama queen of the immune system. Like a diva who demands Percocet for a broken nail, IgE starts a hissy fit over the tiniest things. A speck of pollen grazes a pore and six fire trucks' worth of histamine show up, making the area hot and itchy. And then you scratch.

In eczema, the chicken comes before the egg; it's the scratching that produces the rash, and not the other way around. If you don't scratch the rash won't develop, a hypothesis proved in the 1930s in what I can only assume was an excruciating experiment on a young boy who was duct-taped down and stuffed full of allergens.

In this, eczema is a parallel of hypochondria. It's the symptom—the itch—that produces the disease, and not the other way around. Ultimately, there would be no underlying disease if you didn't respond to the prick of the excessive IgE. Nothing would happen if you could just control yourself, if you didn't get yourself all worked up, just left things alone.

Whatever. I want to scratch. Here's what happens when you scratch: you wreak havoc on the cornified envelope. This sounds like a taco shell but is actually the outer layer of the skin, and in eczema sufferers it gets ragged and red. It's also known as the horny layer. It probably goes without saying that these sorts of double entendres abound in dermatology, the study of flesh, which, until fairly recently focused mostly on syphilis, anyway. Syphilitic skin conditions made up such a large portion of the cases dermatologists saw that dermatology and syphilology were a single discipline until the 1950s, when widespread use of penicillin made syphilis rare, and dermatologists began to focus on more pressing matters like acne and wrinkles. But if your dermatologist graduated from medical school before then his diploma will certify him a syphilologist, and you can only imagine how proud his parents must have been.

Dermatology itself is a fairly new science, dating back just over two hundred years. It seems strange that it should be thousands of years younger than, for instance, *surgery*. After all, skin is the largest organ, the one that, when sick, is the most visibly so; and the one that can normally be treated topically rather than, say, with amputation. But in fact this is exactly what happened. The answer to "Want to check out this rash?" is nearly always no, and it wasn't until the turn of the nineteenth century that anyone got around to studying them with any real determination.

Eczema itself has been around a lot longer, though it's hard to say since when. Because rashes weren't even classified until the late 1700s, eczema tended to get lumped in and confused with conditions normally prefaced by the phrase "the heartbreak of": psoriasis, ringworm, pox, and syphilis. Throughout history it's routinely been mistaken for its look-alike, leprosy, a disease that really did nothing for your social life. For this reason medieval eczema sufferers were sometimes forced to wear a special beaver-skin hat and carry bells to warn others of their approach. You have to wonder how the gene ever carried on.

The word itself is ancient Greek and means "to boil over." Eczema even shows up in the Bible, where it's named as a defect that disqualifies you from the priesthood. It's a red flag imprinted right on your skin, alerting the tribefolk that something's not quite right. In Deuteronomy it's given as one of the punishments for not following the commandments. In my case, it's the punishment for enjoying tomatoes, strawberries, fudge, red wine, hot showers, wool sweaters, or central heating.

It's hard to say what will set it off, and something that didn't bother you at all yesterday may wreak havoc today. Some allergists explain this phenomenon with the "rain barrel" theory. Over the course of time, they suggest, your exposure to allergens adds up, and when the barrel is full—when your body has reached its cutoff point—each drop spills over in the form of an allergic reaction. You literally get sick of things. I got a rash. My sister got a runny nose. With allergies, familiarity breeds contempt.

This has always struck me as odd. How strange that your body should instantly decide that something as innocuous as dust or strawberries is deadly, and come after it with a full-blown histamine attack. I'd understand if I developed hives doing something that was actually bad for me, like sniffing paint or deep-frying butter. But why go nuts when I do something as innocent as apply the wrong hand cream or breathe near an elm tree?

Allergies are an autoimmune misfire. In a sense, they function like your relationship with your siblings. You're constantly attacking your own flesh and blood for no good reason. Vicky and I fought because we were bored, because she couldn't breathe and I was itchy, because there was nothing on TV and the sound of each other's voice made our ears bleed. Then we turned on our parents, and the extended family came next. Familiarity breeds contempt.

In this I was without peer. No one caused as much disruption in my house as I did; no one was as qualified. Eczema sufferers are experts in irritation. Eczema is, essentially, chronic poison ivy, a condition from which it's medically indistinguishable. Imagine having poison ivy every day of your life. Always having something under your skin, you know how to get under others'. I might spend the morning needling Vicky for control of the remote, criticizing her outfit until she returned to the closet in a fit, or systematically scarring her possessions. By lunch I'd be stirring up conflict over the soup, why does she get to pick the soup, we had Chicken and Stars yesterday, I'm sick of it. Dusk would come and it was time to get on her case about whose turn it was to do which chore, and if things didn't go my way I might hand the dog something she loved, her favorite shoe or book or stuffed animal, and let him have his toothy way with it. And when she gave me what I had coming, I'd dissolve in tears, because this is part of eczema, too, being thin-skinned and sensitive. Maybe it's metaphorical, or maybe it's just that being in a hot itchy body makes you feel fragile and prickly, but things tend not to roll off a back that's covered in dermatitis.

It's in no way life-threatening but it sure is annoying, the eczema. Over the years I've tried everything to get rid of it. I have been on steroids more or less continuously for my entire life, the long-term use of which carries certain side effects I have to not think about or I will never sleep again. I have swallowed fungi and microorganisms and mysterious musty gelcaps proffered by hippies. I have spent a month—well, a week, but it felt much longer—on a mercilessly limited macrobiotic diet. I have enrolled in experimental drug studies. I have soaked in baths of olive oil, avocado, and mayonnaise, which did nothing for my skin and even less for my social life. "What's that smell?" friends asked. "Are you wearing *salad dressing*?"

I have eradicated my home of mites and installed air filters. I have meditated, visualized, wished. It always comes back, occasionally getting so bad that I have to sleep with mittens duct-taped to my hands.

Even this isn't much help. Over the years I have learned to remove, without waking, whatever preventative shackles I may have donned before bed, freeing myself to spend the rest of the night happily raking the rest of the skin off my body. It is not unusual for me to scratch myself so hard I leave bruises. It seems appropriate that the disease is caused by a misfire of antibodies: it does, in fact, leave you feeling pretty anti-body, uncomfortable in a skin that is constantly provoking you to attack it.

I never know what the morning will bring. Besides the somatoform symptoms I conjure from thin air are all the very real eczema scars. Raw knuckles and scabbed knees are the norm, but sometimes my savagery surprises even me. A few years ago I woke up in a Kafka story and found I'd been transformed overnight into a lobster. Apparently I'd clawed my whole face into an eczematous mask, and now it was bright red from ear to ear and chin to hairline.

Usually this sort of thing subsides after a while, but as the day progressed it appeared to be getting worse. In high school I'd turned orange; now, it appeared, I was moving along the color spectrum. I hated to think what might be next. A hepatitis yellow? A cyanotic blue?

In high school the cause had been an overdose of carotene, but this time, who knew. The damage was so extensive it took me a while just to figure out what it was. Usually eczema arrives in small, bumpy patches. This was an uninterrupted sheet of it, smooth and tight, hot to the touch and painful. It was a profound tomato red, deeper than a sunburn. It looked very much like I'd applied rouge to my entire face. This was the makeup strategy favored by the alcoholic lady hobo in my neighborhood, and it lent her a certain sassy charm. On me it just looked weird.

Not long before, this very thing had happened on my favorite show, *Sabrina, the Teenage Witch*, the saga of a miniskirted high school sorceress. Sabrina's best friend Valerie had burped in the middle of a presentation, and Sabrina had used magic to ease her embarrassment. Apparently this violated some sort of witch rule and now there was hell to pay. An unfortunate public intestinal event followed and Sabrina's face stayed claret until she learned her lesson, which was either to be honest, or not to eat raw vegetables for breakfast, I forget.

I was hoping for quicker fixes, but nothing helped. Ice baths just made it tighter and drier. Steam treatments made it hotter and itchier. Medication didn't do anything. Lotion made it feel better for the thirty seconds it took my skin to absorb it, at which point it became even more dry and tight and painful, and I'd apply still more, again and again and again and again.

The next day it was worse, and the day after that, worse still. It stung at all times. Showers were unbearable; my face felt like it was being deep-fried. The only thing that eased the burning was a thick coat of Vaseline. This was less than ideal for several reasons. Now I was not just red, but shiny. Vaseline is fairly tacky, and things tend to get stuck in it. My face would pick up things like hair, lint, and crumbs, making me look, by the end of the day, like one of those macaroni-and-glitter collages pre-schoolers make for Mother's Day.

It just got worse and worse. Three days in, I started to molt. Like most eczema sufferers, I tend to shed, leaving such a trail of DNA evidence in my wake that a life of crime is completely out of the question. Even on a good day, I am a squall of skin flakes, and now I was upgraded to a blizzard. The skin flakes became trapped in the Vaseline, and the overall effect was like Christmas tree flocking.

The funny thing about having a flocked, glistening lobster-red face is that everyone feels compelled to inform you that you have a flocked, glistening lobster-red face. Everywhere I went, people weighed in, as if this was something that might have escaped my notice, or that I might have ascribed to bad lighting or unflattering colors.

My reply began to vary as my patience wore out. "I seem to be having an allergic reaction" gave way to "I got steam-burned freebasing." Two days later it was a dismissive wave and a shrug. "The doctor said it's highly contagious, but what does he know."

Normally I shop to cheer myself up but it was clear this

would only make me feel worse. I imagined the shop clerks recoiling in horror, steering me away from the turtlenecks and toward the door, snapping shut cosmetic samples with a glare. "I know we say we can match foundation to any skin tone, but you've got to be kidding me."

Friends were full of suggestions. Because I live in Northern California they were all for things like homeopathic tinctures, acupuncture, aromatherapy, and Reiki. It could have been worse—drinking your own urine is sometimes prescribed—but they were unpleasant enough. One friend led me to a holistic Web site that convinced me the flare was caused by a chemical imbalance in my diet. I was consuming too much acid, and it was leaking out my skin. What I needed was a carefully calibrated balance of acids and bases. For some reason this meant a diet of sweet potatoes, a regimen I kept up for four whole days before getting so sick of it my own urine started sounding like a refreshing change, and gave up.

I should have just gone to the doctor, but for some reason I was embarrassed to. What was stopping me, ultimately, was Old Testament superstition. In the Bible, you get the disease you deserve, a sty for an eye. Skin diseases tend to be punishment for the sins that should leave you shamefaced, and more often than not they're committed against siblings. It's the Mark of Cain. Cain gets his for killing his brother, Miriam hers for gossiping about Moses. And this, like eczema, ran in my family. In general, we get along, but there were a few longstanding internecine family feuds, some bad blood in the bloodline, here and there. My grandfather—who was, in fact, named Abel—had fallings-out with his own brother that lasted for years.

Vicky and I were more like Jacob and Esau, Esau ruddy like me—his nickname was Red—and Jacob, the younger sibling, favored by Providence, who usurped Esau's birthright for a bowl of chili. In my own family, none of us much care for Tex-Mex, so the exchange was different, and more protracted, but the outcome was the same. Despite my grasping, Vicky had gotten my birthright. She'd been mistaken for the older sibling since elementary school. She was taller than I, more popular, more competent, the risk taker, the first to dive in pools I'd dip my toes in years later. Driver's license, first date, first arrest: she reached all the milestones of adolescence years before me. Even our bodies thought she was the older one. It seemed like a horrible biological betrayal, but she'd completed puberty by the time I was just starting it. I'd traded my birthright not for food but for a lack of it, for the eating disorder that kept me prepubescent until college. Esau have I hated, Jacob have I loved.

Showing up at a doctor's office with my red skin felt like coming in with hairy palms, or a face that had gotten stuck that way, or a shampoo bottle up your rectum; you'd brought it on yourself, and everyone had a pretty good idea how. I know it doesn't really work that way, that people don't bring disease on themselves, but deep down, we all believe some people deserve what they get: that asshole boss who got rectal cancer, the bilious neighbor whose gallbladder has to be removed, the pubertal breast cancer I fully expected but somehow escaped.

I was certain my dermatologist was going to deliver a censure. If it wasn't for moral lapses or commandment-breaking, it would be for some frankly bad lifestyle choices that weren't helping my skin a bit. I didn't eat right, didn't sleep enough, drank perhaps too much; nothing illegal, but nothing that would make my parents proud. The doctor would look at my skin and instantly know, like the priests in Deuteronomy, that I'd been behaving shamefully, and banish me to live outside the city gates until Providence had pity on me and made me whole once again.

When you wake up with a red face, it's hard not to read allegory into it. And, in fact, I had plenty to be embarrassed about. Not long before, my paternal grandparents had died, and over the previous few months we'd been distributing their things. This can be a hard time for any family, often involving restraining orders and court-ordered mediators. Ours had actually gone very smoothly, but even when everyone is civil and kind, it's hard and painful work. When there are shifts like this, roles need to be renegotiated. You have to figure out who you are and how you fit in the new family dynamic. If you're defined by your relation to others, who are you when those relations are gone? Our grandparents were the axis around which the rest of us pivoted, and without them, we all found ourselves unsure of our roles. My father was no longer a son, my sister and I no longer grandchildren. I'd always been the good but immature one, my sister, the bad and grown-up; I wasn't quite sure who we were now.

I was still, however, a jackass. I'm ashamed to recall the

drive to the cemetery, my aunt behind the wheel, quietly con-
templating the loss of her father while I rode in the backseat
shouting along with the radio, "Rock! and! Roll! Hootchie-
Coo!" It wasn't that I wasn't sad. I'm just easily distracted. I
am, in every sense, skin-deep. And this, too, is a facet of the
eczema, the ability to focus on one little thing while ignoring
the larger, more important ones, the entire world boiled down
to a pair of itchy, itchy hands.

Oh, those itchy hands. I missed my grandparents very
much, of course, but was also secretly pleased to get my hands
on a few items. For the last few years of their lives I would
catch myself, while visiting them, taking inventory, mentally
fingering their possessions. While chatting politely on the
couch, I'd be thinking how great that coffee table would look
in my living room, how that painting belonged over my love
seat, that chrome clock on my nightstand. I'd briefly be horrified by myself, but then my mind would wander, and I'd start
thinking about where I'd store the Noritake.

At one point, my sister admitted she did the same thing.
"It's okay," she said. "It's only natural. It doesn't mean that
we don't love them. And I'm calling dibs on the Art Deco
torchiere."

Because I was the closest relative with access to a truck, a
great deal of their things did, in fact, end up at my house. The
torchiere, and the painting, and the clock, the Chinese trunk,
the green velvet armchair, the vanity bench, the engraved silver
coffee urn, the jewelry boxes and the jewelry inside: I'd gotten
all of it.

My sister got a purse, and I got an angry phone call.

"Why did you get everything? Gah! You don't even *like* Art Deco. Gah!"

When we were kids and we both wanted something, we would do the logical thing and destroy it. If one of us couldn't be happy, neither could. That's exactly what happened here. It wasn't deliberate, but within a matter of months most of the heirlooms had been ruined. Guests dropped the highball glasses, the cat soiled the furniture, I sent the delicate china on one-way trips through the dishwasher and stored the first-edition books in direct sunlight.

It's to my family's great credit that no one sat me down and called me out, though it is a fact that at the holiday dinner that year Vicky announced, "In case anyone hasn't noticed, I'm the good daughter now."

This would take a little longer to iron out. The red face, however, ended up being pretty simple. There was no sermon, no condemnation of my moral flaws, no heart-to-heart about my role within the family. "It's just a bad flare-up of your usual eczema," the doctor said, when I finally went to his office, and handed me a prescription for a more powerful steroid. I applied it in the clinic bathroom as parents hustled their children away from my weeping sores, and by dinner that night my face was returning to normal.

The upshot of the whole thing was that I ended up enrolled in a drug study. It was an experimental ointment from Japan, originally developed to prevent organ recipients from rejecting their new body part. I was to apply it twice daily and keep a diary of any side effects.

There was a strange one. When you drank, it made your face burn and sting and flush red. It was like topical Anabuse, and the social drinking that normally oiled family gatherings became impossible for me. Thus, another side effect: I stopped being such an asshole. I did not grasp or needle. I gave my sister presents for no reason. I let her have the last Danish. I did not call dibs, did not wreck the night for everyone else, did not run roughshod over those I loved most. Eventually, that side effect wore off; eventually, the eczema came back, and once again I would scratch indiscriminately, lash, draw blood. But for one brief shining moment, I was unblemished, intact, jointed, whole.

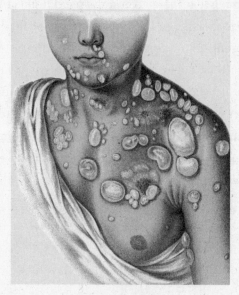

Fig. 13. Pemphigus

14.

Ta-ta

✿

The day before Thanksgiving, my mother called me in a state.

"It's the damn turkey," she grumbled. "I just got a breast this year because there's only going to be five of us, you won't eat meat, and your father and I are dieting. You want to guess how much this cost? Forty-eight damn dollars. Next year I'm stuffing a Spam instead. I'll say this, though—it's *huge.* Eight pounds. I wasn't going to invite the Martins because who wants to deal with them, but I don't know, with all this meat, maybe I should."

On the other end of the line, I was having trouble mustering awe. Eight pounds. Big deal. Earlier that day, I had learned, to my horror, that my own breasts weighed even more. I had gone to see a plastic surgeon to discuss a breast reduction. A hypochondriac with too much time on my hands and a taste for expensive procedures, I'm used to doctors turning me down, but the surgeon hadn't even blinked. "You need this surgery." He'd frowned, taking in the sagging wall of flesh. "This looks like ten pounds of breast tissue here."

Ten pounds. I had more breast tissue than the turkey, a creature whose sole purpose in life, like some poultry play-mate, is to roll around in feathers and be chesty. It is bred to do nothing else. Turkeys become so top-heavy that the bird the president so generously spares each Thanksgiving normally dies a few weeks after the holiday—it is too busty to live.

My condition wasn't fatal, but it was, by now, annoying me to death, causing all kinds of conditions that sent me scurrying in a panic to neurologists, orthopedists, and pulmonologists. Besides all the hypochondriac symptoms, there was a whole host of very real and very unpleasant breast-induced ones. I'd had a neckache for two years running. My shoulders and arms were always sore, occasionally growing so painful and stiff that I couldn't lift them. Some days it felt like I was wearing a lead T-shirt. I couldn't exercise. Well, I could. But I didn't want to, and who could blame me? The slightest bit of aerobic activity caused bouncing that drew alarmed looks. I could stick to weights, I suppose, but what was the point when you looked as bad as I did in workout gear?

What was the point if you couldn't breathe? I got winded climbing out of bed. The weight of my breasts put pressure on my chest wall that made it difficult to breathe deeply, or even normally. When I leaned forward, I couldn't inhale at all, and if I rolled onto my back in my sleep, I woke up gasping. I could breathe easily only when I was propped up on a hillside of pillows. It also helped if there was a stack of magazines and a bag of Fritos.

It was probably just as well I didn't exert myself. Hygiene was enough of a problem as it was. That's a lot of skin to have all mashed together. It's a perfect breeding ground for all sorts of microorganisms, and every time I took off my bra I was overwhelmed by the smell of yeast cakes. I was plagued with rashes, skin tags, and pimples that frequent showers couldn't help. Some women affectionately call their breasts "the girls"; I called mine "the microbe farm." Because of their size, I could not actually see my breasts' underside, but I would not have been surprised if they hosted a colony of truffles. Things were a mess on the surface, as well. Wide and shelflike, my breasts functioned as a sort of crumb catcher, and there was usually a healthy sprinkling of food debris across my shirt. "You've got something, ah, something on your front there," people helpfully pointed out, but I'd stopped worrying about it years ago.

What I couldn't adjust to was the look. Although in real life I'm a lumbering troglodyte, in my head, I'm a pixie, and the breasts just didn't fit my Tinkerbell self-image. They certainly didn't fit with the rest of my body. My proportions were all off. I'm very short and fairly petite, and my breasts dwarfed all my other features. My head appeared especially tiny by comparison. I tried to compensate with fluffy hair, but it still didn't look right. It was a weird distribution of mass, the majority of my flesh gathered in a ginormous lump on my front. With no backside to balance it out, I felt like one of those cheap chocolate Santas, all the action on the front, the back flat as a board.

The front, though. It has always puzzled me that large breasts are compared to melons. In reality, they look much more like eggplants, long and pendulous. Mine reached nearly to my waist. When I heard about the "pencil test"—an assessment of perkiness in which you place a pencil under your breast and pray the breast is not saggy enough to keep the pencil in place—I was eager to see what, besides pencils, my breasts could actually hold. I went from pencils to playing cards to CDs, stopping only after I successfully held up a VHS tape.

That could be handy, I suppose. It was good to know that if I ever found myself without a purse, I could use my breasts to tote my wallet, keys, and lip balm. I knew a few well-endowed women who did just that. One was a free-spirited hard-partying bride who, lacking pockets on her wedding dress, loaded up her bra instead, reaching in every few minutes to pull out items including breath mints, a marijuana pipe, a lighter, and eyedrops.

The downside of this convenience is that you look like you're carrying the contents of an entire head shop even when you're carrying nothing but your own rack. You look bulky. "You're not fat," friends always told me, sympathetically. "You just *look* fat." I thought they could find a nicer way to put it, but they were right. A size eight, I wasn't model-thin, but I certainly wasn't obese. Oh, but I looked it. A doctor I'd consulted several months earlier about my persistent shoulder pain had made me cry when she suggested my only problem was that I needed to lose weight. Losing weight, I knew, wouldn't help. Even thirty pounds thinner, a weight at which I do not menstruate, I hover around a D. And, like hip-hop's overweight lover, it's a heavy D. Breasts comprise primarily breast tissue, an incredibly dense and weighty material, not fat. They are not the pillowy marshmallows of imagination, but sacks of wet sand, and they cannot be worked off. Ten pounds of wet sand strapped to my chest twenty-four hours a day. No wonder I didn't want to go to the gym.

My breasts just didn't match the rest of my body. They didn't even match my personality, having arrived after my self-image was already pretty much set. Due to a combination of hormone-disrupting adolescent eating disorders and unfortunate genes, they'd come very late, showing up without warning when I was nineteen. There's nothing more embarrassing than entering puberty your sophomore year of college. It's bad enough when the whole world takes note of your new boobies at thirteen, but at least the acne, braces, and bad clothes serve as a diversion. But at nineteen, there were no distractions. I was nothing but breasts, lots of breasts, inflating my now-too-small school sweatshirt like a cotton fleece balloon.

I was mortified. My Intro Lit class was reading *Gulliver's Travels* that semester and the description of a nursing Brobdignagian had made me cringe in recognition: "I must confess no Object ever disgusted me so much as the sight of her monstrous Breast, which I cannot tell what to compare with, so as to give the curious Reader an Idea of its Bulk, Shape, and Colour. It stood prominent six Foot, and could not be less than sixteen in Circumference. The Nipple was about half the Bigness of my Head, and the Hew both of that and the Dug so varified with Spots, Pimples, and Freckles, that nothing could appear more nauseous." Oh, it was just awful. We were reading about me. Could everyone tell we were reading about me?

Worst of all was the fact that everyone acted like it was my fault, as though I'd brought on my breasts on by kissing boys, or by wishing for big ones in my secret heart of hearts. People looked at me funny. Mostly they made eye contact with my nipples, but when they looked up I could detect a hint of accusatory dismay, a look of "What did you *do?*" It was most awkward with people who'd known me for a long time. When I ran into old high school classmates, the response was invariably an uncomfortable, "Wow, you've changed. I mean, you've *changed*," their voices registering blame and alarm.

Surely they couldn't think I'd done this on purpose. I hated it. If some body part had to become enormous overnight, why couldn't it have been something more useful, like a tennis racket–size hand, or great big bat ears? Why giant breasts?

They got bigger and bigger and made me more miserable every year. I don't know why I hadn't seen a surgeon earlier. Breast reduction is major surgery, but it's not especially risky or newfangled. It's true that I tend to imagine the worst, but I'd researched it and it seemed safe enough. It is, in fact, one of the oldest operations there is, dating back to the fifteenth century. Oddly enough, it was first done on men, to treat the floppy man-boob phenomenon we find no more attractive today. The modern breast reduction technique was developed in the 1920s, a good forty years before the modern breast augmentation, and within ten years it had become widely accepted as a medical and social necessity. Magazines were full of stories of young girls who'd had their active lifestyles and marital opportunities restored after the miraculous procedure. Have the surgery, they suggested, and in no time, you'd be pinned to a handsome young engineering major.

I'd been mulling a reduction for years. I suppose I was afraid of all the things that could go wrong: infection, scarring, botched shaping, nerve damage, the rare-but-possible outcome of death. I knew one woman whose reduction had resulted in a sepsis that had turned her entire left breast an extraordinary greenish-black. I was appalled. Sure, my bulk forced me to wear nothing but dark slimming colors, but at least the breasts underneath were a nice healthy pink.

What finally got me was the dexterity problem. By the time I was thirty-three, the weight of my breasts had started wreaking havoc up and down my arms. When I typed, the pinkie and ring finger of my left hand often couldn't keep up, and sometimes they couldn't type at all. These are the two fingers I use to type "ass"—a word I need to type at least a dozen times a day—and this was a real handicap. Shortness of breath, chronic pain, a Willendorfian figure—all these things I could put up with, but giving up profanity was too much. That was it. I made an appointment.

So now it was the day before Thanksgiving and I was in a plastic surgeon's office, parked in front of an informational video that taught me, one, that everybody pronounces "areola" differently, and two, that many, many things could go wrong. Besides the list of things that had kept me from seeing a surgeon before now, there was a whole host of complications I'd never even imagined. There was, for instance, "nipple death," a phrase I hoped I'd never have to hear again. I left telling the doctor I'd think about it.

The next day, Thanksgiving, my family gathered around the giant mass of poultry. My mother was right—it was huge. We had more guests than she expected, but they still only managed to eat a fraction of it. That did it. As soon as the long weekend was over, I called the doctor and chose my surgery date.

The next step would be the pre-op office visit, the highlight of which was a topless photo session. I'd looked at hundreds of these "before" pictures while debating the surgery and felt there was a lot of room for improvement. Starkly lit and poorly styled, shot from the neck down, they invariably showcased the subject's flaws: split ends, old tattoos fading to blue, Italian horns, and feather earrings, all of it so terrible that the giant saggy breasts seemed like the least of her problems.

I'd been hoping my "before" picture might turn out a little better than the norm. If it turned out especially well perhaps I'd include in my photo album, or send it out as a holiday card. "Breast Wishes!" the caption might say. But in the end, I bungled it, and simply added more ugly to the archive. I'm the one with bad posture and three inches of tights poking up from the top of the skirt with the broken zipper.

The rest of the office visit was basically a fitting session
with measurements and notations, only instead of a smart herringbone the fabric was my own saggy skin. I was being taken
in. The doctor showed me where my new nipples would be,
about two and a half inches higher than they currently were.
At my initial visit, he'd done the same thing, and it had seemed
to me that my new breasts would sit squarely on top of my
clavicle. This new measurement seemed reasonable. The are-
olae would be reduced from the size of English muffins to
quarters. An anchor-shaped incision would be made on the
underside of each breast to remove the excess tissue, leaving
me with a pair of jaunty red nautical-themed scars that would
eventually fade to pink.

The end result would be a perky little 36C, a size I'd settled on after spending several weeks staring at women's
chests. Friends, relatives, elderly nuns: no one was spared my
penetrating gaze. Companions started to avoid going out with
me. "Oh, cut it out, will you?" my best friend pleaded. "You're
embarrassing every woman here. Well, except for the 34B
with the graying brush cut, who's mouthing you her phone
number."

A 36C it was. It would be a reduction of three or four cup
sizes. I don't know what my actual presurgery size was as I
refused to buy anything larger than a 36DD, continuing to
wear that size even as the elastic groaned and the clasps flew
off, my breasts spilling over into my armpits and up toward my
shoulders. Because my new breasts would have to be large
enough to accommodate my existing pedicle, the stalk of tis-

sue that includes the blood vessels and milk ducts, a C was about as small as we could reasonably go. Because I would also get a lift, it would be a high C.

Once the pre-op business was taken care of, there wasn't much to do but wait. As the surgery grew closer, friends and family rallied round. I was grateful but embarrassed. Sure, I was having the surgery for orthopedic and pulmonary reasons, but breasts have their sexual overtones, and it was a little like having your loved ones support you through a testicle tuck or a penile enlargement.

Still, it was very sweet. My aunts very generously threw me a breast reduction shower, choosing the theme of "Rack 'Em!" instead of "Rally Round the Sag" as I'd suggested. I received a couple dozen bras, one of them weirdly covered in black hair. "Oh, sorry about that," my cousin said, grabbing it from me. "The dog was wearing it for a little while." Later, I repeated this story to her brother. "Oh, yeah," he said. "We all tried on your bras and took pictures. I look really nice in the blue flowery one, by the way."

After I washed them, I was excited about my new bras, but I was a little more ambivalent about the prospect of my new breasts. As the surgery date loomed I grew more and more wary. Should I cancel? Maybe I should cancel. Sure, I couldn't breathe or feel my hands, and I hated the way my breasts looked, but I was still, quite literally, attached to them. We'd had some fun, my breasts and me. There was the time we smuggled a two-pound bag of M&M's into the movies, and the time we provided shade to an overheated child. There were all the years we'd kept people from noticing my other figure flaws, like my flat behind, my thick waist. We'd had a good run, all right.

But now that was all coming to an end. It was a little sad. The surgery meant saying good-bye to a part of myself: ta-ta, ta-tas. Even my loved ones were sort of sorry to see them go. I saw my sister a couple weeks before the operation, and as she left she bid her farewell to my chest. "Okay, let's go," she said, holding her hands up like she wanted to honk them.

"Are you kidding?" I'd asked.

"No, come on, this is my last chance."

"They're going to be the same breasts, only smaller," I'd said. "You wouldn't grab my butt to say good-bye if you'd know I was going to lose weight, would you?"

"Oh, no, I would," she answered thoughtfully. "In fact, why don't you turn around right now?"

I suppose it was nice to have my family's support. The night before the surgery my parents came over to art-direct my digital "before" photos. "Wear the green shirt, honey," my father urged. "You look especially bad in that." These were terrible, terrible pictures. I'd been entertaining the thought of canceling the surgery up to the last minute, but these photos were enough to convince me that it was truly a necessity. My HMO would probably cover the surgery on aesthetic grounds alone. I went to bed thinking about baby T's.

Well, baby T's and death. I was a little nervous about the next day's event and the unlikely, but possible, chance of everything going wrong. I liked my life, and wanted very much to continue living it, and I especially didn't want to die this way. I'd been given a brief rundown of what would be taking place in the OR and it didn't seem like a good way to leave things. My arms would be on blocks and my legs would be in quilted silver clot-preventing boots, like a Bond girl awaiting rescue. Periodically they'd have to sit me up, topless and unconscious, to gauge for evenness. There would certainly be blood, and there would probably be drool. I'd heard that sometimes the departing soul looked down on the body it was leaving and I did not want this image to be the last thing I saw. Somehow I managed to push this out of my head and think about congressional redistricting instead, and the next thing I knew I was out cold.

This is exactly how I'd spend the better part of the next few days. "We have more drugs than you have anxiety," the nurse said when I arrived at the hospital the next morning. In no time I was swimming in Versed, a fuzzy nectar that made me want to tell stories that began "This one time, on spring break . . ." while the doctor marked me up with a Sharpie. There was more Versed, and some other drug that was even better. Then the counting backward, like in the movies, and then the nice long nap.

The next thing I knew I was in Recovery, where I entertained my parents by turning disturbing shades of gray, white, and green. Later, my father told me that I'd looked worse than any patient he'd ever had. But I think this may have had less to do with the surgery than with my complexion's aversion to fluorescent lights, since my high school photographer had told me the same thing.

I went home that night, groggy and aching and confused, and spent the next several weeks recuperating at my parents' house. Having my meals prepared and being able to spend all day in my bathrobe made me feel like I was at a spa, and soon I was pretending I was at Rancho Parento. Rancho Parento, truth be told, was a pretty crappy resort. There was no cable, and the magazine selection was wanting. "I'm not sure you're in any position to complain," my mother muttered, bringing me my midmorning snack of sliced apples and part-skim ricotta. "Oh, hush," I replied. "Isn't it time for my hot stone massage?"

Yes, I know, but hadn't I been through a lot? I was exhausted and nauseated and too sore to move. I'd been told I would feel some "discomfort" for a few days. I felt like I'd been flayed, which, in fact, I had. I'd been carved up like a turkey.

For this there was Vicodin. I'd used Vicodin to treat boredom in college and remembered it fondly, but it was a little less effective on fourteen inches of sutures than it had been on ennui. It made the pain just bearable but it did not, as it once had, make me want to hug strangers.

Though everything seemed to be proceeding normally, I was anxious and needy, certain that everything was going wrong. I forced my family to run through reassurance routines so often it started to feel like we were reading from a script.

"Do you want to perform 'Is My Nipple Falling Off?' this morning or will it be 'Bruise or Blood Clot?'" my mother wondered aloud. "How about 'Is It Permanent Nerve Damage?' We haven't done that one in a while."

But day by day, things got a little easier. After a week it was time for my post-op checkup and the first look at my new breasts. "Looks great," the doctor said, placing me before a mirror for the big ta-da moment, just like when you get a haircut, only with hematomas, scabs, and sutures.

There they were: Betadine-yellow and a little bit bruised, the left noticeably fuller than the right, red scars running all over, the ragged, uneven nipples staring at me like the eyes of a particularly abused stuffed animal. These were not my breasts. I was looking at someone else's breasts, and right now this someone had some fucked-up breasts.

"Very nice," I said, and then asked to lie down.

It was just a lot to take in. Walking was suddenly difficult because I seemed to be in someone else's body. I'd been told I'd feel light, but I felt like I might float away. Unexpected things were suddenly, surprisingly off. When I smiled I felt a tug on my newly taut nipples. From now on, apparently, I was going to be very, very happy to see you.

Everything had changed. My weight distribution, my posture, my breathing—it was all completely altered. Later that day I tried on shirts for the first time. With a nearly flat chest and shoulders that suddenly seemed broad by comparison, I looked like a boy. But maybe that was because my hair was clumped into a Prince Valiant do and I needed a lip wax.

I didn't recognize myself. I'd often dreamed about this very thing. In my fantasies I made a wish and woke up an ecto-morph. At first I'd be shaky on my elegant coltish legs, but in no time I'd adapt and delight in my elegant tapered fingers, my concave belly, my willowy height. In reality I staggered and lurched in this body that felt so different. How could it be so different? In the end the surgeon had taken out less than we'd expected: only three pounds. It just made such a change. Three pounds, a medium-size mass, the same weight as the human brain.

My family was wondering if the surgeon had taken out three pounds of brain tissue instead. My thought processes were dif-ferent, too. I am normally a somewhat spacey person but in the weeks after the surgery I was Anna Nicole Smith. I was also weepy and depressed. I'd been warned that post-op depression is common and was prepared for a few blue days, nothing that couldn't be cured by a couple Manhattans or a good celebrity scandal. I hadn't expected this airless black hole of despair. I am, normally, a happy if neurotic person, but now I was given to teary outbursts and gloomy pronouncements. At the dinner table, my father would ask me to pass the salt and I'd answer, "Well, it's all just pointless, isn't it, since we're all going to die, anyway?" My mother and I would be watching game shows and I'd collapse in tears during the speed round. "They're all just so stu-hu-hu-pid," I'd sob. "All that work getting on the show and they're just going to go home with car wax."

Overnight, I'd been transformed into a moody brat. Per-haps I should have seen this coming. Getting breasts signals your entrée to adulthood; losing them, it seemed, signaled a return to puberty. Suddenly I was thirteen again, insolent and lazy, living with my parents, relying on my mother to drive me around, fighting the urge to write bad goth poetry and send it to Robert Smith. This time, my melancholy was caused by drugs, and in my teens, by hormones, but the upshot is the same, chemicals changing your body in some ways you like and some you don't.

No wonder so many societies have ceremonies to mark the occasion, some celebration and magic to make the transition easier. In New Guinea, girls welcome their breasts by shoving nettle leaves in their vulvas. Nkoya girls are draped in beads and commanded to dance. Here we basically do the same thing, plus or minus a Mardi Gras float and *Girls Gone Wild* film crew.

As an adolescent, a college student, it had felt like my breasts had changed overnight. This time the transformation was as short as a nap; four hours later I woke up and everything was different. Getting used to them took a little longer.

But slowly, gradually, things got better. I adjusted to my new body. My energy returned. The rigid hams in my bra settled and softened and evened out, the scars faded and flattened. After a couple months, I could take care of myself, and I went back to my apartment, to live, once again, like a grown-up. More or less.

Some things were different. Others were not. I knew the surgery wouldn't transform my life completely, but because it did solve some problems that one would imagine would be entirely unrelated to cup size—the uncooperative pinkie finger, the shortness of breath—I couldn't help hoping it would fix all my problems. It would shrink my feet to fit my pinchy suede flats, and help me make that call to my accountant I'd been dreading. It would teach the cat to stop biting, and get the wine stain out of the couch. Or it would transform me so completely that I wouldn't mind these small irritations, these little bumps in the road.

Except for the little bumps, I'm the same. But now, when I get exasperated, I have the lung capacity for the most satisfying sigh. And when I fold my arms across my chest in annoyance, they reach.

Fig. 14. Lupus Serpiginosus

15

Calculus

✿

Contrary to popular belief, smaller breasts do not, however, make you any more intelligent. Like many liberal arts majors, I favor the right side of my brain. To the extent that I can think at all, I can't help thinking I favor the right more than most. My aptitude for math and science is so weak that I sometimes think the left hemisphere is missing entirely. I routinely forget whether the numbers on the TV go up or down, and sometimes get so confused by the remote I have to call friends for help. It's possible I'm a little retarded.

The only time numbers make sense to me is when they concern health. Then they please and reassure me, imposing order on the randomness of disease. This is the reason I like the actuarial roteness of medical office work, and I've done it most of my adult life.

For a while I worked in a gastrointestinal lab. I don't even like to be in the same room when my cat uses his box, but it didn't take long to adjust. The nurses frequently neglected to close the door during procedures, and I grew used to the sounds, the wet slurping, the swears and apologies from the uncomfortable, embarrassed patient.

What disturbed me was the oldies station they played to distract the patient from the fact that heavy equipment was being shoved up his rectum. When you're having a colonoscopy the most innocuous songs can have an ironic effect. Bob Seger's "Fire Down Below" is an obvious one, but the Atlanta Rhythm Section's "I Am So Into You" takes you by surprise. In a disco, the Bee Gees' "How Deep Is Your Love" is a romantic ballad, but in a GI lab it begs for a "g" before that last word. "Smooth Operator," "Back in the Saddle Again," even Beethoven's second movement—the music doesn't distract so much as taunt.

But I had headphones, and I got used to the smell. Occasionally something would come out of a patient that was so disturbing it would send the nurses, GI nurses who did this every day, dry heaving into the halls, but most of the time it wasn't too bad. What unsettled me were the occasional, unexpectedly pleasant scents. Once, the entire department was overwhelmed by a pervasive cloud of butterscotch. Someone must have brought in a flavored coffee, but all I could picture was a landslide of sundae topping sludging out of a patient's behind.

This was not a job at which an imagination served you well. I suppose that's part of the reason I liked it. There was the occasional surprise, sure, but generally you knew how the day would unfold, an orderly procession of backsides. The repetition makes it less scary. Here, every day, we saw the very worst the body has to offer, and conquered it with tedium and time limits. Your misery was scheduled from two o'clock to three o'clock, and then we sent you on your way. It would be an unpleasant hour for everyone, but the patient would go home with answers, a care plan, and some Tylenol 3, and we'd all feel good about ourselves.

Eventually I was moved to a different department, but this was fine by me; my new office had its own cot, and the work was interesting. Here I helped handle supply for surgery, burn, and trauma. I liked medical jobs because they allowed me to order bodies, organize and manage them, but in this position I was *ordering* bodies. Like, literally, out of a catalog, ordering prosthetics and parts.

The shopping list was always fascinating. Some days it might be my job to order skin, a surprisingly complicated business that required follow-up questions like, "Do you just want cadaver tissue or should I get the kind they grow from foreskins?" You could even order a kit that would let you grow skin yourself from harvested DNA for an exact donor match. The cost was prohibitive, but I couldn't help wanting some for crafts. Imagine the things you could do with sheets of your own skin. It would make the most personal valentines ever.

Never in my life did I receive such great catalogs. The best were from companies that specialized in medical training mannequins. These offered a mind-blowing assortment of bloody severed plastic limbs, gynecological exam models, trauma victims in bloodied tracksuits. There was even a life-size geriatric mannequin which thoughtfully featured "interchangeable male/female genitalia" as well as "enema capability." I'm real and I don't think I have either of those features.

What charmed me most was that the mannequins all had names. You could practice giving hypodermic injections to Annie Arm or Pap smears to Pelvic Patty. You could bring home Terry Trauma or Mr. Hurt Head, with his squinty eyes and fake-looking hair, his face, according to the catalog, "cast from an actual victim of a road accident." What extraordinary gifts these would make, what lovely coffee table pieces. The fun you could have every time someone asked you to lend them a hand.

This was what I brought home: disgusting anecdotes and curiosities. My friends worked in food service, and they were good for leftover mozzarella sticks; my contribution was stories that made you not want to eat them.

Then the HIPAA privacy laws were enacted, and I could no longer repeat my best ones. They're part of a trend in medicine in general, to overorganize, overlegislate, all these rules and regulations a charm against the inevitable mistake. My father loathed them. The last years of his career were a morass of rules and paperwork, which took the joy out of practicing. Not long before he retired, his clinic was taken over by a large health-care conglomerate, and with this came policies and procedures, binders and meetings and memos telling him how to do his job. Some, I suppose, ensured better care; others seemed pointless. It was probably a good idea to require pre-op surgical marking and consent forms, but legislating desk accessories was a bit too much. When told his office could host no more than one framed photo of his family, my father responded by inviting the family to sit for a portrait with all four of us flipping the bird.

The surgeon's motto is "Frequently wrong, but never in doubt." If you weren't completely sure of yourself you could never do the things the job requires, slicing into the innocent belly, its owner asleep and perfectly trusting. I can't imagine what that feels like. The hypochondriac brain lacks a surety function; I doubt everything. Gravity, air, whether I'm still alive or just *dreaming* I'm alive—these things are obvious and concrete to most people, but to me they're just abstract ideas that are up for debate. You can't live this way, of course, so I've learned to take the big things on faith. The rest of the time, I rely on rules and equations, formulas and schedules.

Some obsessive-compulsives get hung up on numbers, trapped in counting routines they can't break, but for me they've just been a comfort and guarantee, a sequence I can interpret unambiguously. It's ten a.m., my heart rate is 68, it's 60 degrees outside with an 80 percent chance of rain: well, then, I'm probably alive, and I'd better take an umbrella.

For people like my father, the practice of medicine is an art. But for the rest of us, the less confident or capable, it's simply a numbers game. Your general health is defined by the string of digits that make up your vital signs: heart rate, blood pressure, temperature, and respiration. Numbers predict what happens next. If your white blood cell count goes over a certain number, you get antibiotics; below, antiretrovirals. It's odds: it's the chances that you'll get this or that, and if you do, that this treatment will help or won't. It's measures and schedules. Every sensation can be monitored and timed. Relief will come at half past ten, with the next dose of Fentanyl. Torture will be squeezed between two o'clock and three o'clock in the GI lab, and then it will be over. It's an equation, a formula, that even someone like me can figure out.

Numbers are certainly much easier than names. Nurses often call patients by their room numbers: 708 needs wrist restraints; 722 shat on his floor. Names make it too personal and painful. Sometimes I think of the real Mr. Hurt Head, the nameless trauma victim, and wonder what happened to him. Did he survive? And if he didn't, does his family know the mold was cast? Someday, will his wife renew her CPR license and be confronted with the latex likeness of her dead husband? And then it stops being funny: the bad plugs become pathetic, the stricken expression, just horrifying.

IN MEDICINE, "calculus" refers not to math but to a hardening: calcium deposits that form stones in your kidney, adhere to your teeth, line your arteries. Medically, calculus is, literally, a hardening of the heart. The calculus of substituting numbers for names and unknown outcomes performs the same trick, forming a callus over the tender parts.

The numbers are exactly that, numb-ers that help you distance yourself, help you believe it won't happen to you. The tumor becomes an unlikely probability, the swollen lymph node an abstract algebra that will be solved down to zero by x amount of radiation. It's so tidy, really. This is why I like the work. I am an accountant of the body, reducing the messiness of mortality to seven white digits on a blue plastic card. This, I like. This I can do.

Which is probably why I later ended up working for another hospital owned by the same conglomerate that bought my father's clinic, writing up the very policies and procedure manuals that plagued the end of his career. Perhaps unsurprisingly, I worked for the department that made sure all the policies were followed. When things deviated, I would write a report, and assign it a number. The young girl with third-degree burns who became agitated and extubated herself becomes incident #24156; the elderly man who arrived with the bedsore, #24157.

I'd get there by nine o'clock. For the next four hours I would impose order, just as I had as a teenager. By one o'clock I would be done, and I'd go home to eat the same lunch I always ate. By then, the cookies and cottage cheese I liked in high school were no longer manufactured, so instead, every day was vegetable soup and toast, whole-grain, because I've spent time in a GI lab, and I know where refined flours can lead. I'd chew each bite five times. At 1:45 the plates were in the dishwasher. At two o'clock, I'd sit down with my tea and the TV remote, because you can only read Jane Austen so many times.

Instead, I'd do more equations. From two o'clock to three o'clock equaled channel 13, and from three o'clock to four o'clock equaled 5. I'd watch neurofibromatosis patients on *Sally Jessy*, followed by bipolar horror stories on *Oprah*. It was okay; it wouldn't happen to me. All was right with the world, and everything was in order. I'd done the math; the odds seemed in my favor. And today, at least, the colonoscopy happened to somebody else.

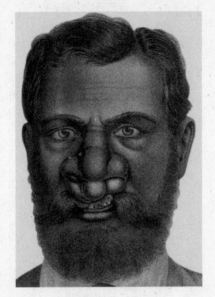

Fig. 15. Rhinoscleroma

16.

Gut Reaction

✲

Sometimes, however, the colonoscopy happens to you.

By my early thirties, I'd had no shortage of embarrassing conditions, from sores and scabies to self-administered injuries done in the service of something truly stupid. Once, reaching for a frozen pizza at the grocery store, I'd pulled my groin so badly that I was bedridden for days; and another time, I gave myself a massive black eye when I hit *my own head* with a beer bottle while dancing. But nothing was quite so humbling as the GI revolt that came on, almost without warning, at thirty-four. This was a new low. I had, quite literally, hit bottom.

I'd developed irritable bowel syndrome, a condition with a name so inelegant that even the ads for the drugs that treat it—ads that explicitly mention diarrhea, constipation, bloating, and gas—refer to it only by its initials, in the hopes you might think it stands for something else. Fish odor syndrome, alien hand syndrome, and cretinism all get called by their full names, but irritable bowel syndrome is really just too embarrassing to say. It's a fitting name for a condition that lends its sufferers not one bit of dignity, whose symptoms can include such gems as watery stools and anal mucus and a little something known as chronic idiopathic diarrhea. It's a sorry business.

It was a while before I figured out exactly what business this business was. I am quick to call the doctor when I think my symptoms will lead to massages or muscle relaxants, but when they're likely to result in anal probing I put it off until I see blood. And when that happened I ignored that too, ignored the cramping and the nausea and a very long list of indignities that cannot be mentioned in polite company.

It's not actually true that hypochondriacs call their doctors at the smallest sign. It's true that we want to, but over the years the condition trains you to wait a while before picking up the phone. Nine times out of ten my brain tumor/kidney failure/broken ankle really does go away before I make it to the doctor's office, and I've learned to wait a bit for the symptom to dissipate. Sure, this had been going on for what, a year or two now, but it could still turn out to be nothing. It was probably nothing. Maybe nerves. Or maybe I should just stop having root beer and corn Bugles for breakfast, that could be the problem right there.

Here's what finally got me: once again, I looked fat. IBS causes a strange swelling, and my abdomen would bloat up with alarming speed, regularly fluctuating as much as four inches in just a few hours. It was very inconvenient, leaving the house in a size eight dress only to discover, by the time I got to the party, that I was now a size fourteen. The gain was all in my belly, and strangers regularly asked when I was due. I took to buying maternity clothes, becoming particularly attached to an elastic-paneled number I referred to as my eatin' skirt.

It seemed a terrible irony, this. I'd been hoping to be pregnant in the next year. Now here I was, my belly filled with air instead of baby, an empty balloon. My IBS had come on in the wake of a scorched-earth breakup. It's unusual to develop IBS in adulthood with no history, but it's not unheard of, and a breakup is just the sort of thing to do it. A terrible irony, again: if he's the asshole, why are you the one shitting blood?

IBS is not a disease but a syndrome, the diagnosis you get when everything else is ruled out. This means going through a truly humiliating battery of tests, including something we'll gently call "specimen collection"; twice, if you, like me, get lazy and sort of drop the ball in the middle of things and then have to go back and do it all again about six months later; three times if you, like me, then end up *spilling your specimens on the floor.*

I have collected my urine, worn Holter monitors, and offered my naked, jelly-smeared self to all matter of diagnostic scanners, but never have I been subjected to something as unpleasant as home stool collection. It sounds relatively harmless, like shopping for Danish modern high chairs. In actuality it involves making a deposit into a toilet attachment that resembles a plastic cowboy hat. You then use a cute little spatula to transfer the contents to a variety of different collection jars, all with different chemical preparations that can't be cross-contaminated. The vials and solutions will make you feel like you're conducting an experiment, like you're a mad scientist in the lab, and will remind you of the chemistry kit you pined for and which your cousins actually owned, which you once used to run a chemical analysis on lasagna. Which is, in fact, what you're doing now, only it's lasagna that has spent a day or so in your digestive tract and been transformed into something entirely less appetizing. It's all you can do not to throw up or spill it, and of course you end up doing both.

So you go back to the hospital to get yet more collection vials and repeat the whole process again, and then you have to throw the vials in a bag and get on a bus and pretend that you are not going across town with your own poop in your purse and drop it off at the lab and just pray that the people who are there getting tested for perfectly unembarrassing conditions like syphilis and anal herpes don't see you hand what is very clearly three vials of your own feces to the lab tech. And we won't even touch on the difficulties of disposing of a *now soiled* plastic cowboy hat that you have to get out of the house immediately, because it is *now soiled* and of course it won't fit in your trash can and you wouldn't want it there anyway, so the mission ends up requiring multiple plastic bags and an incognito run to an unlocked Dumpster in what is surely a serious violation of some health department laws as well as all that is good and decent.

And then the fun won't be over because after they've run the samples and determined that you don't have a parasite or a bacterial infection you will get to come in for a sigmoidos-copy that will make home stool collection seem like baking cupcakes, like petting bunnies. From six o'clock the night before you will be on clear liquids—which, inexplicably, includes Jell-O (neither clear nor liquid) but not vodka (both). Because you won't eat Jell-O and your procedure isn't scheduled until the late afternoon the next day, you get to fast for twenty-two hours. You will, however, be permitted, in fact commanded, to drink a bottle of super-lax soda, a saccharine-y sodium citrate refresher which is not bad for the first sip before the aftertaste kicks in, at which point you realize you'd rather consume your own specimen than finish this. It is like drinking gasoline. It is so distasteful, in fact, that it will take you nearly an hour to finish it and you'll have to play games and trick yourself to get it down. And that's when you'll be seized by a paroxysmal need to empty the contents of your gastrointestinal tract, urgently, like a distressed plane dumping fuel over the ocean. You can actually hear this, your gut rumbling like a troubled engine.

The next morning you will get to drink another bottle for breakfast, then self-administer two enemas as a finale. As a result you'll spend several hours curled up sweatily on your bath mat, the unhappiest patch of real estate on this earth, clotted with cat litter and hair, but you will be too weak and cramped to move. And then, finally, you will drag yourself onto a bus and just pray you can get across town before your colon expels its last in some horrible death rattle and you finally get to collapse on an exam table.

That's when the hose-mounted camera is shoved up your rectum. Because sigmoidoscopies are, apparently, less invasive than the full colonoscopy, you will be unmedicated and awake. You've been told that you will feel some discomfort, some *pressure*, but since the colon does haven't have nerve endings it can't really hurt. This turns out to be (again, literally) a load of shit. You have, in the past, been accused of having a stick up your ass, and now that you actually do, you can see why it might make a person uptight. You've never sat on a scimitar, but you're fairly certain this is exactly what it would feel like. The straightaways are abject misery, but the turns—the colon has lots of these—are so excruciating you feel that you will absolutely die right there. And the worst thing of all is that you can see it broadcast in real time, you're hosting a TV show from your butt, and the only mercy is that it's over quickly and there aren't many viewers.

And when this test turns out negative, too, but you're still plagued by the symptoms we will, again, demur from detailing, although we've just detailed the televised anal assault, the diagnosis of IBS will be confirmed.

At this point you're rewarded with something you badly need, which is Prozac. IBS is a strange disorder, a stomach ailment that's treated with drugs for your brain. For a long time it was believed to be a psychosomatic condition, but current research suggests that it's a real chemical problem, caused by an imbalance of serotonin, like depression (it is, in fact, sometimes called depression of the stomach, and the two often coincide). It's also extremely common, afflicting 20 percent of the population—a very specific 20 percent. For reasons that aren't entirely clear, it affects far more women than men; 70 percent of its sufferers are female.

As far as diseases go, IBS is a fairly new one, a catchall for various gastrointestinal disorders that fit no other clear diagnosis. Because gastrointestinal disorders were so common during the centuries of hypochondriac chic it's hard to say how prevalent it might have been had this been considered a disorder and not the norm, but it seems reasonable to guess IBS would have been epidemic. And a lot more fun: some seventeenth-century enemas were, essentially, hot buttered rum. Samuel Pepys treated his chronic constipation with clysters of strong ale, sugar, and butter, and pronounced himself quite pleased with the results.

Now it's treated with less tasty remedies. IBS is a serotonin malfunction in something called the "enteric system," the neural network that oversees all aspects of digestion. The enteric system is also known as the second brain due to its similarities to the first. It runs on the same equipment, a network of nerves and neurotransmitters that closely resembles the workings of the brain. It also enjoys an unusual relationship with the brain, a sort of dedicated phone line that allows the two to transmit information quickly and easily, which explains why you kept having to run to the bathroom during the SATs. Your gut reaction is often, in fact, quite literal. Brain and bowels are closely linked. It's been theorized that Lincoln's lifelong melancholy was actually caused by constipation (history buffs interested in seeing his last—and apparently rare—bowel movement can view it in a Baltimore museum).

After the sigmoidoscopy has confirmed the diagnosis of IBS you're given a selective serotonin reuptake inhibitor like our friend Prozac, which seems a little like prescribing a martini for a hangnail but you won't complain, because it's a little like prescribing a martini for a hangnail. And the strangest part is that it works like magic, eradicating all your symptoms almost instantly.

There turns out to be a very good reason for this. We think of serotonin as a brain chemical but in fact 95 percent of the serotonin in the body is in the digestive tract, where it acts as a sort of traffic cop. When you eat, serotonin is released into the wall of the gut, signaling the release of digestive enzymes and reflexes that move food through the intestines. At this point the serotonin is normally flushed out by SERT, a serotonin transporter. And this is where people with IBS get into trouble. We're SERT-deficient, so the serotonin accumulates, causing what's effectively a digestive traffic jam. But SSRIs regulate serotonin, and the problem is solved.

The whole thing makes me think of prison, in part because untreated IBS chains you to a toilet, but more because it uses the same tools to communicate: shit. In prison you use what you have and often the only weapons you have are the ones you, well, make yourself. My cousin had taught in a jail and for a while prison slang became something of a family hobby. We were delighted to learn most of it turned out to have fecal referents. We were fascinated by the concept of "gassing," the fairly routine practice of throwing your waste at guards, and captivated by the "Dirty Sanchez," which involves a shit-smeared upper lip as a finale to sex. My personal favorite was the "Drive-by Hot Carl." I never learned if this was a real thing or just something my cousin made up, but from what I understand it consists of pooping in a sweat sock and then using it to beat someone, and if that's not genius I don't know what is.

The other population that communicates with its own feces is, of course, babies, and as I lay on my bathroom floor, I was thinking about the likelihood I'd ever have one, and the last time I got to pretend I did. I was fourteen. A family friend was having major surgery, and my mother offered to take her year-old baby for a week. Ostensibly, it was to give the poor woman a break, but I think it was at least in part because my sister and I were teetering on the brink of puberty and my mother thought a week of round-the-clock babysitting would make effective birth control.

"You girls are going to be in charge," she announced. "I'll take care of her while you're at school, but the rest of the time she's all yours. And you better do a better job with her than you've done with the dog. By which I mean, if you let her shit on the neighbors' lawn, you'll no longer be allowed to live in this house."

Predictably, the experiment had ended badly, with much diarrhea (the baby's), vomit (mine), and confusion (universal). "Well, that was a disaster," my mother muttered, after the baby had gone home. But it hadn't been a disaster, really. We'd returned the baby in the condition we found her, more or less, and my mother's plan did work: neither Vicky nor I got pregnant.

I still haven't, and as I waited for the second enema to take effect, I wondered if the baby-as-contraceptive plan had worked too well, if I picked partners who are unlikely to stick around, or picked fights when it looked like they might, a pattern that ends with me curled in a comma around a toilet as sodium citrate rumbles through my gut.

The last watery spasms shuddered through my system. Then a wave of relief followed, and it occurred to me I could do this, whatever *this* entailed: enema or spinsterhood or sickness or whatever was coming next. Baby or barren, together or alone, I'd be all right.

Besides, I already had a baby to take care of. She was lying on the bathroom floor, wearing my clothes. Instead of an umbilical cord, she was tethered to an enema hose, and she was counting her blessings, secure in the faith that everything would be okay. Someone would come along to clean things up, make things right. And if they never showed, if she stayed alone, she'd be well enough, either way.

Fig. 16. Compression of Arteries

17.

End Note

✿

At the end of *The Hypochondriack,* James Boswell confides that writing about his hypochondria has cured him of it. And at the end of this, my hypochondria seems to be in remission, though I suspect this has less to do with semicolons than sigmoid colons. Ultimately, I think, it was the IBS that put an end to things. So to speak.

IBS is what prompted me to get on Prozac. Prozac was a miracle in a gelcap: a pill that really did solve all my problems and cure all symptoms. It knocked out the residual obsessive-compulsive tics I didn't realize I still had. It soothed the pricking and quieted the anxiety. On Prozac I could do things I never could before, that made me too uncomfortable or nervous: talk to strangers. Drink coffee. Wear clothes that fit. A pill can't make you learn to accept your body, but it can make that body easier to accept: the freshman fifteen I'd kept for seventeen years disappeared. Also, I'm pretty sure my feet shrunk a half-size.

Here was the miracle drug I'd dreamed of as a child in my

cough-syrup-soaked nights. It's true that SSRI's don't work for everyone, and they can make some people worse, but I got lucky. Prozac cured the IBS, as well as the brain cancer, kidney failure, diabetes, and gout. The imaginary illnesses evaporated. Recently doctors have begun to think that the drug might be effective on hypochondria, and early studies bear this out: 75 percent of hypochondriacs improve dramatically when they go on an SSRI.

I certainly did. I didn't stop getting sick entirely—right now I have an impressive case of yoga-mat foot rot, and these little sores on my tongue that make it impossible to eat salt and vin-egar chips—but I'm not particularly concerned about either one. I haven't had a hypochondriac episode, a real one lasting more than five minutes, since I started the little green pills.

Or maybe, like I said, it's just because I got really good cable.

WHEN I WAS WELL ENOUGH, as things happened, I stopped being alone. Not long after I started taking Prozac I met my intended. He's the best thing that ever happened to me, a bet-ter man than I deserve, who patiently holds my hand when I'm trying to claw a patch of eczema off my wrist and overlooks the residual effects of the IBS. "Maybe you'd like to do your burp-ing on the porch," he'll gently suggest, but he doesn't leave the room. And although our respective DNA is so overloaded with the same conditions we should probably consider adoption, when he asked me to marry him, I could trust my gut reaction, and say yes.

It's true that we're similar in some ways that don't bode well for the family's long-term health. "You both eat nothing but soda and candy bars," friends point out. "It's nice that you were made for each other and all, but you should probably think about taking an organic chef as a sister wife. If she can't change your ways at least you'll have someone to take care of you when you guys are forty-five and need your colostomy bags changed every three hours."

But I don't think it will come to that. I don't plan to come down with anything, imaginary or otherwise. And if I do, if I don my satin bed jacket and take, once again, to my boudoir like Camille, I know my Armand will be at my side.

"You're weak," he'll say, taking my hand.

"No, no," I'll answer, just like in the film. "Strong. It's my heart. It's not used to being happy."

Appendix

❊

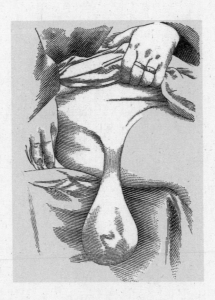

Fig. 17. Molluscum Fibrosum Pendulosum

1. Please bring me to the infectious-disease specialist.

   Por favor, tráigame al especialista contagioso de la enfermedad.

   Bitte bringen Sie mich dem ansteckenden Krankheitspezialisten.

   Пожапуйста принесите меня инфекционному специаписту бопезни.

   Amenez-moi au spécialiste contagieux de maladie, s'il vous plaît.

2. I believe I have a parasite.

   Creo que tengo un parásito.

   Ich glaube, daß ich einen Schmarotzer habe.

   Я думаю что у меня ест кищечный паразит.

   Je crois que j'ai un parasite.

3. What, exactly, is the certification process for medical doctors in this country? Is it reliable?

¿Qué es, exactamente, el proceso de la certificación para médicos en este país? ¿Es seguro?

Was ist genau das Bescheinigungsverfahren für Doktoren in diesem Land? Ist es zuverlässig?

Что, точно, является процрессот свипетепъства ппя врачи в зтой стране? Пействитеиьно пи зто напежно?

Qu'est-ce que le procédé de certification pour les médecins dans ce pays? C'est fiable?

4. I'd like to schedule a colonoscopy.

   Yo quiero planificar una colonoscopía.

   Ich móchte eine Darmspiegelung planen.

   Я хочн наметитьи копоноскопия.

   Je voudrais planifier une coloscopie.

5. Hello! I think my spleen is infected.

   ¡Hola! Pienso que mi bazo se infecta.

   Hallo! Ich denke, daß meine Milz angesteckt ist.

   Привет! Я думаю, что моя зпоба заражена.

   Bonjour! Je pense que ma rate est infectée.

6. How long is the waiting list for a kidney in your country?

   ¿Cuán largo es la lista de espera para un riñón en su país?

   Wie lang ist die Warteliste für eine Niere in Ihrem Land?

   Какой дпины? пист ожидания дпя почки в вашей стране?

   Est-il longue, la liste d'attente pour un rein dans votre pays?

7. Where is the ICU?

   ¿Dónde está la UVI?

   Wo ist der Intensivstation Einheit?

   Где итр?

   Où est l'USI?

8. It appears that my goiter is growing larger.

   Aparece que mi bocio crece más grande.

   Es erscheint, daß mein Kropf größer wächst.

   Кажется, что мой зоб становится бопьшим.

   Il paraît que mon goitre grandit.

9. Antibiotics are available over the counter here? I would
   like to apply for citizenship.

   *¿Los antibióticos están disponibles sin receta aquí? Querría
   solicitar la ciudadanía.*

   *Antibiotika stehen zur Verfügung ohne eine Verordnung
   hier? Ich möchte Staatsbürgerschaft beantragen.*

   Антибиотики поступны без предписания здесь? Я хотеп бы
   просить гражданство.

   *Les antibiotiques sont disponibles sans prescription ici?
   J'aimerais faire une demande de la citoyenneté.*

Ten Horrible Diseases and the Chances
You Already Have One of Them

1. *Amyotrophic Lateral Sclerosis (ALS)*

A degenerative neurological condition and pretty much the worst disease ever. Five thousand people are diagnosed with it every year in the United States alone. It's almost always fatal, and cruelly progressive, eventually leaving you paralyzed and unable to breathe on your own. Most cruelly of all, it can leave your mental processes intact, so you know exactly what's happening to you. It starts small, with muscle twitches or soreness. How scary is that. This is the disease that keeps me up nights.

2. *Huntington's Disease*

Also the worst disease ever. Similar to ALS in its progression, it will render you unable to walk or talk, and unlike ALS, to think, which might be a blessing. There is no cure and no particularly good treatment. It affects one out of every ten thousand Americans. Irritability is an early symptom. How are you feeling now, cranky pants?

3. *Necrotizing Fasciitis*

Utterly terrifying. You can get it from a pedicure, a scratch, or nothing at all. It's lightning fast: bacteria eat your flesh, and then you die. If you live you'll probably lose a limb. It can happen to anyone, and does, to about fifteen hundred people each year in the United States. Look for a red patch. Any red patches? You better hope not.

4. *Hantavirus*

One, you get it from rat poop, which is incredibly gross; and two, it's a *hemorrhagic fever*. About thirty people get it every year in the United States, and 38 percent of them die. Don't breathe in rat poop.

5. *Ebola*

Another hemorrhagic fever, and a far more deadly one, with an 80 percent fatality rate. About fifteen hundred people have gotten it worldwide. You saw *Outbreak*. You don't want this.

6. *Myiasis*

You know what myiasis is? It's when your flesh is invaded by parasitical maggots that can later hatch into flies. It's more common in Africa and Central and South America, but don't think you can't get it here. Not generally fatal, just completely gross. Also, funny name (pronounced "my ass is," as in, "my ass is crawling with worms").

7. *Plague*

Thought this one was extinct? Think again. Black death is alive and well, producing its painful characteristic buboes and killing people all over the world. Though more common in Africa, about fifteen people get it in America every year.

8. *Leprosy*

Now known as Hansen's disease, the biblical favorite is still around. About one hundred fifty people contract it each year in America alone, though goodness knows how—95 percent of the population is naturally immune. If you get it you must be really, really unlucky, or, per the Bible, a big sinner. The good news is it's curable. The bad news is if it's left untreated, it causes extensive tissue destruction.

9. *Alien Hand Syndrome*

Also known as anarchic syndrome or Dr. Strangelove syndrome. Not actually one of the most horrible diseases ever, but one of the most interesting. The hand operates independently of the brain, as though it were being controlled by a remote entity. The hand can perform complex operations, just not the ones you ask it to. It usually occurs after brain surgery or stroke. Not fatal, unless you choke yourself with it. And people have.

9a. *Lesch-Nyhan Syndrome*

I just remembered there's this other weird disease that makes you attack yourself as if you had no control over your hands. Lesch-Nyhan syndrome is a rare genetic condition, affecting only males, that compels sufferers to harm themselves. If left unrestrained, they will do things like gouge out their nose, eyes, and facial bones. They also tend to bite off their fingertips, and frequently chew off their lips.

10. *Rabies*

Sure, it's pretty rare—affecting about one American every year—but you sure don't want to be that one. Symptoms include convulsions, mania, paralysis, respiratory failure, and weirdest of all, hydrophobia, an aversion to water so strong that just looking at it will cause throat spasms. Oh, and it's pretty much always fatal and excruciating.

11. *I know I said ten but I just found out about an eleventh: Morgellon's disease.*

Doctors aren't even sure if it's a real disease yet, but if it is, it's new and terrible. Here's what happens: *filaments grow out of your skin.* You develop a sensation that bugs are crawling under your skin, then lesions show up, and these *fiber bundles.* It's the strangest thing you've ever seen. Because sufferers also tend to exhibit symptoms of Chronic Fatigue Syndrome, OCD, and Attention Deficit Disorder, researchers aren't sure if it's a psychological delusion or an actual infectious disease. *Filaments! Out of your skin!*

Your Health Horoscope

AQUARIUS: You're a high-powered go-getter. You always get what you want, as long as that doesn't include living a long life. When you get cancer, it's going to be as aggressive as you are. You're probably already stage IV. Better get your affairs in order.

PISCES: You're the classic wishy-washy water sign. Is it chronic fatigue syndrome or lupus? Fibromyalgia or MS? Who can decide? You'll probably need a lot of tests. We hope you have good insurance.

ARIES: Hey there, hothead. When's the last time you had your blood pressure checked?

TAURUS: You're stubborn as a bull, which probably means your doctor will never convince you to get your prostate examined. Just so you know, prostate cancer affects 30 percent of men. It will probably leave you impotent and incontinent, but maybe it won't kill you.

GEMINI: Hi, twin sign! Did you know that some people are born with a parasitic twin inside them, absorbed in the womb, that they don't even know is there? It's not really dangerous, but now that you know about it, it'll probably drive you insane.

CANCER: In the stars? It's in the *name.* You should probably schedule that biopsy right now.

LEO: Me, me, me. Leos just love being in the spotlight. Here's a fun fact: narcissism is a clinical condition. It's not curable, either.

VIRGO: Virginal Virgo, did you know that you can catch all kinds of venereal diseases even if you're not sexually active? You can get chlamydia from handling turtles, and gonorrhea can be spread just sharing towels. And that thing about oral sex not really being sex? You'll change your mind once you catch oral syphilis.

LIBRA: Even-tempered Libra never panics. And that could just be your nature, but it could also be an adrenal condition. I wouldn't worry, though. Lots of people manage just fine with only one kidney.

SCORPIO: You're a passionate Casanova, flitting from fling to fling. Here's something to keep in mind at your next makeout session: kissing is a great way to catch mononucleosis, meningitis, strep throat, and herpes. Isn't that romantic?

SAGITTARIUS: You're open and generous. I sure wouldn't want to sit next to you on a plane. What say you cover your cough? And that looks like scabies on your wrist, so how about not touching my armrest, either?

CAPRICORN: "Oh, don't worry about me," says reserved and modest Capricorn, "I'm sure it's nothing." Yeah, right. Hope you enjoy that double pneumonia.

DISEASES THAT WOULD MAKE NICE NAMES IF THEY MEANT SOMETHING ELSE

Chlamydia

Listeriosis

Porphyria

Rosacea

Roseola

Rubella

Scarlatina

Shigella

Syphilis

An owl sat in a tree, watching a vulture feeding upon a deer carcass. "That's a bad idea," said the wise owl. "Who knows what that deer died from? You could catch something terrible. You should eat safe foods, like these nice clean worms I have right here." The owl was right about the carcass. It was, in fact, infected with a terrible bacteria that made the vulture writhe and seize. But what the owl forgot was that eating even safe foods can be dangerous if you don't chew properly. The owl was so distracted by the vulture's convulsions that it choked on a worm, and within an hour both owl and vulture were dead.

There once was a cheetah who was afraid of melanoma. "All these spots," he said. "Any one of them could be skin cancer." So he checked and checked each spot for malignancies every single day. This took all his time and attention, and when he developed a sore on his paw he didn't notice it until it was septic. The paw soon became gangrenous. The cheetah didn't die, but he did lose that leg, which was probably worse.

Deep in the forest, a fastidious badger lived next door to a family of raccoons. The badger didn't like his neighbors. Raccoons have all kinds of terrible habits. They eat garbage. Some of them even smoke. These particular raccoons also used IV drugs and had sex without condoms. One day the raccoons had a party and then chucked all the empty cans into the badger's yard. "You raccoons are going to catch something awful, and you're going to deserve it," said the badger. "You're filthy, your eating habits are terrible, and it's only a matter of time before you contract something fatal." The raccoons remained fine, but the badger died later that spring. It turned out he had a terminal liver condition. Sometimes that's just what happens.

A giraffe had a sore throat but he was too scared to go to the doctor. "That's nonsense," said his best friend the cat. "There's no such thing as a scaredy-giraffe. Besides, it could be something serious. You're my best friend, and I couldn't go on if you got sick and died." But the giraffe didn't listen, and he died five days later from meningitis, which wouldn't have been fatal if he'd been treated in time. Meningitis is incredibly contagious, so the cat went to the doctor too. It was too late. The cat and giraffe are buried next to each other now, but like everyone else, they died alone.

FRUIT/TUMOR COMPARISON CHART

	FRUIT	TUMOR
Raisin	*Prognosis*: Raisins themselves are pretty harmless if you're human, but completely toxic if you're a dog. They cause acute renal failure in certain breeds.	*Prognosis*: A raisin-sized tumor is typically stage I, normally highly treatable. It's still cancer, though. Good luck with that.
Plum	*Prognosis*: Unripe plums contain the same chemical compounds as cyanide, and if you ate three hundred in one sitting you'd probably	*Prognosis*: If your tumor is plum-size there's a decent chance it's a lipoma, which is good, because it's benign; and gross, because it's composed

die. Otherwise, they're pretty harmless unless you choke on the pit. Fun fact: The Japanese term for syphilis is "plum disease," because of the plumlike appearance of syphilitic sores.

of fat, like a big scoop of Crisco.

Grapefruit

Prognosis: Grapefruit's high level of vitamin C has some health benefits, but the fruit can be harmful when consumed with certain medications.

Prognosis: At grapefruit size, a tumor is typically stage III (no node involvement) or stage IV (nodes involved). Prognosis varies, and the treatment protocol isn't much fun. The good news is you'll have no problem getting a prescription for medical marijuana, which might make eating grapefruit more appealing.

| Watermelon | *Prognosis*: Watermelons are perfectly harmless. However, a condition called "watermelon stomach," so named because the stripes it produces in the stomach lining resemble a watermelon's markings, can cause slow bleeding that leads to anemia. | *Prognosis:* Tumors this big actually exist, and are typically ovarian. Even when they're benign, they can be dangerous, as it's hard to move something the size of a watermelon without dinging organs in the vicinity. Also, they're occasionally filled with fluid, though not, as in college, vodka. |

HYPOCHONDRIA HAIKU

Plantar fasciitis
is more harmful than you'd think.
Even feet can kill.

Dark spot on my arm.
It could be just a mole, but
with my luck, cancer.

Don't worry about
me. I'm sure it's just a cold.
Or, say, pneumonia.

Night comes; sleep evades.
I don't drink coffee. I guess
it's a brain tumor.

Cat sleeping, content.
It doesn't yet know it has
Cat leukemia.

Heart, mysterious.
What secrets lurk inside it?
Fatty deposits.

Symptom-Matcher Insta-Diagnosis

Redness	Sure, it could just be a sunburn, but with your luck, chances are it's necrotizing fasciitis.
Sore neck	Maybe you slept funny. Or maybe you have meningitis.
Tingling extremities	It could just be that your foot is asleep. Or maybe it's the first sign of multiple sclerosis. You should probably get an MRI.
Cough	It's probably just a cold. It's highly unlikely you have lung cancer. Emphysema is pretty probable, though, and tuberculosis is almost a given. When was your last TB screen? Five years ago? Are you kidding?
Runny nose	Have you ever heard of Wegener's granulomatosis? It's pretty awful, and a runny nose

is one of the symptoms. But try not to worry about it. I'm sure it's just your allergies.

Headache Maybe it's just tension. Or maybe it's the Ebola virus. A headache is one of the first symptoms, you know. I bet you're feeling pretty tense now.

Nausea Visited the taco truck again? Maybe you just overate. Or maybe you got hepatitis.

Rash There's no way it could it be AIDS, right? Kaposi's sarcoma? It couldn't be that, could it? No. Probably just hives. Well, maybe.

Depression You're probably just having a bad day. Hey, did you know that depression is one of the first symptoms of rabies? That's pretty depressing.

Perfect health Most people who have coronary artery disease feel perfectly fine.

ACKNOWLEDGMENTS

I'm grateful to the following folks who keep me well but not alone: father Alain, mother Judith, sister Victoria, brother-in-law Chris, and nephew Elliott; the McGraths, especially Peter; the Neffs, especially Maureen; the Clabbys, especially Mary Lou; the Schleichers, especially Miriam; the Zweimans; and friends Angela Hernandez, Amie Nenninger, Stephen Elliott, Ryan Gray, and everyone at 826 Valencia. Accountability Club cofounder Caroline Kraus provided much-needed advice and encouragement. Dr. Cleve Baker was an invaluable resource on the history of dermatology, and provided the book's vintage illustrations. Uncle/allergist Dr. Burton Zweiman generously shared his histamine expertise. Father/surgeon Dr. Alain Traig helped in too many ways to count. Professor Katherine Ibbett was a gold mine of Molière facts. Thanks to Dan Kennedy for being an all-around good guy. Thanks to brilliant editors Megan Lynch and Geoff Kloske, to Sarah Bowlin and Amanda Dewey. Thanks to wonderful agents Emily Forland and Wendy Weil. And thanks, finally, to cure-all Rob Mickey, who makes me feel well, no matter what.